Praise for *Earthrise*

"*Earthrise* provides a great picture of the space program and of Ed Mitchell's personal experiences, from growing up to his education to his military flight experience that ultimately led to his walking on the Moon on the Apollo 14 mission."

———Fred Haise, Astronaut and Apollo 13 Lunar Module Pilot

"Like my fellow moonwalker Edgar Mitchell, I had the opportunity to see the Earth from some 240,000 miles away. I believe this experience will give anyone a changed perspective. This book is a gift to all of us, as it is an honest look at a heroic historical figure and his unique way of thinking."

—Alan Bean, Apollo 12 Lunar Module Pilot

"This fascinating, charming, and gripping book gives us a rare and powerful glimpse into the fantastic life of an Apollo astronaut. Edgar's catching narration—describing his journey, the flight, the fun and exertions of a weightless life in space, the walk on the Moon, and the collection of Moon rocks—makes this book so very absorbing and spellbinding."

———Juliane Gross, PhD, Research Scientist, Department of Earth and Planetary Sciences, Rutgers University

"With each turn of the page, Mitchell's relatable voice speaks to the reader and creates a fully immersive experience—one that is truly out of this world."

—*South Florida Sun Sentinel*

"This book is strongly recommended for all children who are interested in space; as Edgar Mitchell was inspired by stories of Roswell and of Buck Rogers when he was young, perhaps a child who reads this very book will someday fly around the Moon and watch the Earth come up."

—Universe Today

"I've never read an autobiography for children that was this riveting, honest and understandable."

—Smart Books for Smart Kids

"Edgar Mitchell writes in a comfortable friendly way, making this book a natural for a young adult, or advanced child, as well as an easy read for the adult looking to read beyond the cold facts (as told by NASA) of this lunar mission."

—*Seattle Post-Intelligencer*

EARTHRISE

My Adventures as an Apollo 14 Astronaut

Edgar Mitchell

with Ellen Mahoney

Foreword by Dr. Brian Cox

CHICAGO
REVIEW
PRESS

Copyright © 2014 by Edgar Mitchell and Ellen Mahoney
Foreword © 2014 by Brian Cox
All rights reserved
First hardcover edition published in 2014
First paperback edition published in 2025
Published by Chicago Review Press Incorporated
814 North Franklin Street
Chicago, Illinois 60610
ISBN 978-0-89733-541-6

The Library of Congress has cataloged the hardcover edition as follows:
Mitchell, Edgar D.
  My adventures as an Apollo 14 astronaut / Edgar Mitchell with Ellen
Mahoney; foreword by Dr. Brian Cox.
    pages cm
  Audience: Age 12+.
  Audience: Grades 7 to 8.
  Includes bibliographical references and index.
  ISBN 978-1-61374-901-2 (cloth)
  1. Mitchell, Edgar D.—Juvenile literature. 2. Astronauts—United
States—Biography—Juvenile literature. 3. Project Apollo (U.S.)—
Juvenile literature. I. Title.

  TL789.85.M57A3 2014
  629.45'4—dc23

                              2013037858

Interior and cover design: Sarah Olson
Cover images (clockwise from top): Earth seen from the Moon and
Edgar on Moon with flag, courtesy NASA; Edgar standing on wing
and sitting on pony, courtesy Edgar Mitchell
NASA transcripts courtesy of NASA Historical Reference
Collection, Washington, DC

Printed in the United States of America

Contents

....

Foreword

....

I was 23 months old when Edgar Mitchell walked on the Moon. I watched it live on TV, according to my dad, and perhaps this is one of the reasons why I have always thought—known, in fact—that the Apollo program remains humanity's greatest achievement, despite half a lifetime of engineering and scientific progress.

There are many reasons I know this, and you will read about them all in this book. In purely engineering terms, the goal set by John F. Kennedy in 1961 to land an astronaut on the Moon within a decade was more than ambitious, only 58 years after Orville Wright flew the first powered aircraft. Perhaps it could only have been achieved by a nation founded by explorers: "Ten years to the Moon? I took it as a personal challenge," writes Edgar Mitchell. We have all benefited from the technologies and techniques developed during the Apollo years, in aviation and countless other fields.

But there is a deeper reason to celebrate the spirit of Apollo: exploration is vital to human survival. This simple fact is often overlooked in an age where some see space flight as an unaffordable luxury. The great chemist Sir Humphry Davy made the case for the expansion of our physical and intellectual domain at the turn of the 19th century, just as the benefits of the Industrial Revolution were beginning to emerge. "Nothing is so fatal to the progress of the human mind as to suppose that our views of science are ultimate; that there are no mysteries in nature; that our triumphs are complete; and that there are no new worlds to conquer."

This book is the story of how a young farm boy from New Mexico learned these lessons firsthand by flying to the Moon and looking back at our home planet from a distance of a quarter of a million miles. Edgar Mitchell describes eloquently how his experiences in war caused him to look for a peaceful way to use his piloting skills, and how his flight aboard Apollo 14 changed his view of human possibility and progress. These are two of the most extreme experiences imaginable. The first none of us would wish to share, but the second I personally would have loved, although I am sure it takes a special kind of explorer to climb aboard the Saturn V, to this day the most powerful flying machine ever built.

The most fascinating thing for me about this book is the insight it delivers into the personality of such an explorer, and how that personality changed as a result of a grand adventure beyond Earth. "If only our leaders could see Earth from space," writes Mitchell, "we'd have different economic and political systems here on Earth." I have never had that privilege, but my own experience in thinking about the origins and evolution of our universe and the natural laws that govern it leads me to a similar conclusion. Perspective is the key. It is far too easy for our societies to become myopic, gazing at the ground rather than the stars. Science, engineering, and exploration force us to look upward and outward, and I do not think it is idealistic or cliché to dream of a civilization that values these pursuits significantly more than we do today.

The Apollo program, more than any other human endeavor, demonstrated what is possible when we merge our scientific and engineering creativity with our powerful instinct to see beyond the horizon. Edgar Mitchell's book is a fascinating insight into the mind of one of those explorers, and the story of how his vision for the future was shaped by a voyage to the Moon.

DR. BRIAN COX is a professor of particle physics and Royal Society University Research Fellow at the University of Manchester School of Physics and Astronomy, Manchester, England. He presents various space and science programs on BBC (British Broadcasting Corporation) radio and television, including *Wonders of the Universe.*

INTRODUCTION

. . . .

Trouble on the Far Side

> *"Courage is resistance to fear, mastery of fear—not absence of fear."* —Mark Twain

February 5, 1971, was no ordinary Friday. In fact, it was one of the most extraordinary days for planet Earth. There was a great deal of excitement on Earth, as well as nearly 240,000 miles away in space. Two humans were about to walk on the Moon, and I was one of them.

I was part of the historic Apollo 14 Moon mission along with astronauts Alan Shepard and Stu Roosa. Alan was Commander of the flight, Stu was the Command Module Pilot, and I was the Lunar Module Pilot. As astronauts, we were all part of NASA, the National Aeronautics and Space Administration program in the United States. Stu and I were rookie astronauts and we'd been training for years for this important Moon mission. Alan was already famous all over the world as the very first American to fly into space.

Just five days earlier, an enormous Saturn V rocket had blasted us out of Earth's orbit and into space from the Kennedy Space Center in Florida. And now, as we soared toward the Moon, our home away from home was the Command Module (CM), a large high-tech spacecraft Stu had named the "Kitty Hawk" in honor of the Wright brothers' first flight in Kitty Hawk, North Carolina.

We were so close to the lunar surface we could almost touch it. A few hours earlier, Alan and I had dined on a bizarre-looking breakfast of vacuum-sealed toast, bacon cubes, and lukewarm orange juice. But food was low on our priority list; there were important tasks ahead.

As Stu flew the Kitty Hawk around the Moon, Alan and I carefully pulled on our bulky white spacesuits, which would keep us alive in the treacherous and airless lunar environment. Once we were suited up, we floated through a narrow hatch of the Kitty Hawk and into a smaller oddly shaped mini-spacecraft. This smaller spacecraft was our Lunar Module (LM), which Alan and I would use to fly down to the Moon. I had named this craft the "Antares" after a bright navigational star in the Scorpio constellation.

After we were inside the Antares, Alan and I locked the hatch and took our places at the control panel. If everything proceeded exactly as planned, our spacecraft would land us on the Moon.

It wasn't long before we heard NASA's Mission Control announce, "Kitty Hawk and Antares, you have go for undock!" Located in Houston, Texas, Mission Control was our informational lifeline during our flight, and we were constantly in touch with an important team of Capsule Communicators

(CAPCOMS), engineers, scientists, and medical personnel who were all vital for the success of our mission.

"We're ready to go!" I said.

Full of anticipation, Alan and I undocked the two spacecraft and backed the Antares out into the black sea of space. It felt like being in a small boat that had been set free from a large ship in the chilling darkness of night. But we were carefully and precisely heading toward our destination.

Stu was now completely alone in the Kitty Hawk, where his job was to fly the spacecraft above us as he orbited the Moon. Stu would be busy taking photographs of the lunar surface and keeping a watchful eye as he awaited our return.

Looking at the Moon through the window of the Antares was thrilling and unlike anything I'd ever experienced. I could see the vivid dark and light shadows of the Moon's many craters and its rocky, barren terrain that stretched for miles. It was hard to believe I was so close to the big white orb I'd looked at my entire life.

Although excitement filled the cabin, being onboard this mini-spacecraft was a challenge. It was so small that Alan and I had to stand up for almost everything. We stood up to fly the craft. We stood up to communicate with Mission Control. And we stood up to work and eat.

Our flight plan and descent to the Moon were very specific and highly detailed. After detaching from the Kitty Hawk, we were to orbit the Moon about two times to make sure everything was going as planned and all our instruments were working perfectly. Fortunately, we knew a Moon landing was possible because four astronauts had already walked on the Moon. Apollo 11 astronauts Neil Armstrong and Buzz Aldrin had landed at a site called the Sea of Tranquility, and Apollo 12 astronauts Pete Conrad and Alan Bean had landed at the Ocean of Storms.

Now it was our turn. Alan and I were going to set down our craft in a beautiful area of the Moon called the Fra Mauro Highlands. This would be our celestial home for about two days.

Everything was functioning exactly as it was supposed to, but then something suddenly went wrong. As we flew our craft in a low orbit about 10 miles above the Fra Mauro region, a bright red light flashed on our control panel. The light delivered a straightforward, no-nonsense message: Abort! Abort!

Alan and I were stunned. Why was our spacecraft telling us to abort? Were we supposed to head back and return to Stu? After all this time and effort, was the Antares telling us to give up and go home?

My scientific mind went into overdrive as I tried to diagnose the problem. I quickly realized there were three potential scenarios. One, we would land on the Moon after solving the problem. Two, we would crash on the Moon. Or three, we would abort the mission and return to the Kitty Hawk never having set foot on the Moon.

But we'd flown nearly a quarter of a million miles to get here and we were extremely close to landing. I couldn't imagine failing now.

Alan and I started an intense conversation with our CAP-COM, Fred Haise, in Mission Control. I felt my heart pound and wondered what the NASA doctors thought about my heart rate, which was constantly being monitored. I took a deep breath and focused my mind.

WHAT'S UP WITH THE MOON?

Formed nearly 4.5 billion years ago, the Moon is about 2,000 miles across and has an airless environment with no wind or weather and extreme temperatures ranging from +250 degrees Fahrenheit to –380 degrees Fahrenheit. The Moon's surface consists primarily of anorthosite (the light-colored areas), and its many craters were formed from the bombardment of countless asteroids, comets, and meteorites over time. Some of these craters filled with lava that cooled to form basalt. The dark areas on the Moon are similar to the rocks of Hawaii.

About 240,000 miles from Earth, the Moon is Earth's only natural satellite. It has one-sixth the gravitational pull of our planet and directly affects the continual rise and fall of Earth's sea levels and tides.

The same side of the Moon always faces our planet, and it takes the Moon about one month to orbit Earth. Depending on its position in relation to the Sun and Earth, the Moon goes through monthly phases including: new moon, waxing crescent, first quarter, waxing gibbous, full moon, waning gibbous, last quarter, waning crescent, and new moon. When the Sun, Earth, and Moon are in exact alignment, the Earth blocks the reflected sunlight from the Moon and a lunar eclipse

(continued on the next page)

occurs. A harvest moon is a full moon that is seen closest to the date of the autumn equinox in the Northern
Hemisphere, and a blue moon is the name for the second full moon in one month.

During the Apollo Moon missions, a large cache of
nearly 840 pounds of Moon rocks was brought back to
Earth.

We were told there was a computer malfunction in our
spacecraft and a young computer whiz named Don Eyles
at the Massachusetts Institute of Technology in Boston was
going to help solve the problem. Don had designed the craft's
original computer software and knew the system better than
anyone. In the meantime, Alan and I were directed to continue to orbit the Antares around the Moon and then wait to
hear what to do next.

As we carefully flew the Antares around to the far side
of the Moon, we had a complete communication blackout
with Mission Control. We worried about what else might go
wrong. Would we run out of fuel? Would we be able to solve
this malfunction? Would we make it?

As I looked out my window again, the surface of the Moon
now seemed foreboding and even a bit frightening. Minutes
passed by like hours. But with my long career as a navy pilot, a
test pilot, and now as an astronaut, I felt certain I could handle
what was happening. In fact, I felt 100 percent wired to take
on this otherworldly challenge. I knew that every experience

of my life, step by step by step, from my childhood until now, had prepared me for this moment.

Would Alan and I ever walk on the Moon?

Time would tell.

From Big Skies to Buck Rogers

> "Looking at these stars suddenly dwarfed my own troubles and all the gravities of terrestrial life. I thought of their unfathomable distance, and the slow inevitable drift of their movements out of the unknown past into the unknown future."
>
> —H. G. Wells, The Time Machine (1895)

I was born in a small stucco home on September 17, 1930, in the quiet rural town of Hereford, Texas. Hereford is located in the northern area of the state referred to as the Texas Panhandle. I was the first son of three children, and my grandmother, Josephine Arnold, helped my mother, Ollidean Mitchell, bring me into this world. My father's name was Joseph Thomas, but everyone called him JT.

Some people say everything is "big" in Texas, and as far as landmass, that's true. But as a child, what looked incredibly big to me was the sky, which loomed large above the Texas prairies and plains.

The night sky was a spectacular sight because there were so many glistening stars. Sometimes on warm summer evenings my dad and I would sit on the porch or head out to the nearby farm fields to stargaze. As we walked among the lightning bugs and listened to the hum of the crickets, we'd stare up at the sky and watch for shooting stars. If I were lucky enough and saw one streak across the sky, I'd holler out, "Look, Dad! I see one!"

It wasn't easy to find constellations in the star-speckled Texas sky, but if I tried I could usually find the Big Dipper and the Canis Major formations. And when the Moon was full and looked like an enormous dinner plate suspended in space, I would always look for the Man in the Moon.

Little did I know that one day I would be a man *on* the Moon.

Sparky, Oscar, and a Herd of Herefords

My family moved from Texas to New Mexico in 1935. I was only five years old, and I now had a younger sister named Sandra. The four of us, my mom, dad, Sandra, and I, packed all our bags and belongings into our black 1929 Buick coupe. Sandra and I sat in the car's rumble seat as we headed due west about 170 miles to the small town of Roswell, New Mexico, located in the Pecos Valley.

In Roswell we lived on a small 100-acre farm that had elm and cottonwood trees, roses, a windmill, and a picket fence to keep cows from wandering into our yard. The Berrendo Creek ran through our property and provided us with delightful swimming holes during the rainy season. Our home was a simple brown clapboard farmhouse with a living room, a kitchen that had an icebox and a wood-burning stove, two bedrooms, a sleeping porch, and a bathroom. My mom always grew a vibrant vegetable garden in one corner of our yard. I loved our little home.

The Pecos Valley was an exciting world of rolling hills, prairies, pastures, rivers, streams, caverns, and canyons just fit for adventure. There were always plenty of things to do and places to explore in this rugged but beautiful Southwest terrain.

Over the years I grew up surrounded by many different types of farm animals and pets. I had a Shetland pony named Sparky, and my all-time favorite pet was a small black-and-white terrier I named Oscar. Oscar was a great little dog and would follow me wherever I went—around the house, out to the fields, out to the barn, the corral, or even into town. Oscar's favorite trick was racing across the yard, jumping up onto our propane tank, and then taking a flying leap for as far as he could go. It never ceased to amaze me.

When I was about 10, Dad gave me a steer to feed and raise, and I felt grown up because he trusted me with so much responsibility. At the time I was a member of the local 4-H Club, which was a club for farm kids in the area. The four Hs stood for head, heart, hands, and health. Every year, the other 4-H members and I would take our groomed horses, calves, cows, steers, bulls, lambs, pigs, sheep, and goats to the Roswell County Fair where we'd auction off and sell our livestock to the highest bidders. Although it was always a good time and there were rides like Ferris wheels and merry-go-rounds, the county fair helped introduce me to the cattle business, which was my dad's line of work.

Growing Up

As a boy, my world was one of hot dusty days, wide-open spaces, farmland, fences, barns, horses, and cattle as far as you could see. I grew up in cattle country.

My dad was a third-generation cattle rancher, and along with my grandfather and my two uncles, our family eventually owned a fairly large ranch where about 200 Hereford cows and calves, and a few young bulls, roamed and grazed.

But cattle ranching didn't start out easy for the Mitchell family.

My grandfather lost everything he owned during the Great Depression, which started in 1929 and lasted about 12 years in this country. Grandpa lost his home, his farm, all his cattle, and all his money. It was an incredibly tough economic time for nearly everyone in the United States; jobs were scarce, poverty was rampant, and severe drought and dust storms made farming impossible at times.

But unlike some people, Grandpa didn't give up. He was a clever, hardworking man and started his career all over again working on the Santa Fe Railroad in Texas as a laborer. He worked on the railroad with my dad and my dad's two brothers, Bill and George. Grandpa carefully saved all their earnings, and when he scraped together nine dollars he was able to buy one decent, healthy-looking heifer. It was a small step, but a nine-dollar step in the right direction.

Grandpa then turned around and traded the cow for a little more money so he could buy a few more heifers. By starting small and buying and selling cows, he slowly and methodically built up his cattle business all over again.

Grandpa had a great sense of humor and was spry at an older age. He eventually moved into the business of selling bulls, and his business buddies nicknamed him "Bull" Mitchell. Grandpa would trade his registered bulls to ranchers in return for cows and calves, and then my dad would help feed and raise the cows and calves before taking them off to market to sell.

Typical Farm Days

As a farm boy I was always busy helping my parents with whatever chores needed to be done. I remember many a hot, sweaty day milking cows, fixing tractors, or mowing, baling, and raking the hay. And although we had farmhands, I'd also help with big jobs like grinding up our tough, five foot tall Hegira grain and hauling it off to our feedlots.

Most of the time, wherever I was, I looked like a typical cowboy. I wore a wide-brimmed Stetson hat, a long-sleeved denim shirt to protect my face and arms from the scorching sun, and khaki trousers. While riding our horses, I often wore chaps to protect my legs from saddle burn as well as the thick brush on our ranch. And I usually had on cowboy boots, which made it easy to move my feet in and out of the stirrups.

My younger brother, Jay, was born seven years after me. When Jay was older, he and I would often do our chores together. During the winter months the chores let up a bit, and my homework always came before my farm work. My parents insisted I work hard in school, and this was okay with me because I enjoyed learning new things.

Wild West Roundups

Land seemed to be ever plentiful in the Pecos Valley, and we eventually bought a 4,000-acre ranch near the small town of Hagerman, New Mexico, which was about 20 miles from Roswell.

In addition to our many heads of cattle, we always had a lot of horses. We had big, muscular Belgian horses to pull our feed wagons, and leaner horses like mustangs, quarter horses, and Appaloosas for roping and herding the cattle. The wide-open, grassy plains of our ranches afforded me a lot of land where I could take off and ride my horses as fast as I wanted to go.

Cattle roundups were a vibrant and challenging part of working on the ranch. By the time we were in Hagerman, I'd been riding full-grown horses for many years, and I was very skilled at being in the saddle and racing across the fields to rope the cattle or chase a stray. I loved the speed, the intensity of the work, and being good at moving the herd to where it needed to go. I would move cattle from one pasture to another, to a holding pen for vaccines, a chute for branding, or to a special dipping vat where the cattle would swim through medicinal treatments.

Dad would always let me know when it was time to herd. I'd gallop out to the field and take my place with the other cowboys alongside the cattle. Once we took off, a lot of dust would fly as we used our horses, our ropes, and our voices to get the cattle moving. The cowboys would whistle loudly, yell and hoot, "Hey! Hey! C'mon girl! Yup! Yup!" And when the herd started to take off, it felt like a powerful wave of energy as hundreds of hooves pounded across the plains.

Naturally, it wasn't all fun and games. I remember difficult times like being thrown from my horse, going for hours without much water in the blazing hot sun, and coming across a rattlesnake or coyote on my path.

As our cattle business prospered, my dad and uncles also decided to go into the business of selling large farm machinery to the ranchers in the area. Dad eventually opened a farm machinery dealership in Roswell, and then a second one in the small town of Artesia, located about 40 miles from Roswell. Sometimes during summers or on weekends, I would help out at one of the dealerships and work in the machine shop. I learned how to repair large pieces of equipment such as tractors, trailers, threshers, mowers, hay rakes, and balers by carefully taking them apart and putting them back together.

Working on these large pieces of machinery and learning about their engines gave me an important confidence I would later put to use as a pilot and an astronaut.

Family Time and the Great Outdoors

We had a tight-knit family, and when we weren't busy working we had many happy times together.

Music was always played in our home and was a big part of my life. Mom loved playing the piano, and when I was about seven years old she encouraged me to take violin lessons. Since I was left-handed, my parents had to have my violin reconfigured (from right to left) so I could play it. I wound up playing the violin for many years in the Roswell and Artesia youth orchestras. Later on in junior high and high school, I also took up the viola, piano, sousaphone, and trombone.

It was always great when the entire family piled into our Ford truck to go camping somewhere in New Mexico, Colorado, or Texas. We would usually set up a few tents next to a river or a stream to catch rainbow and cutthroat trout or smallmouth bass. At the end of the day we'd make a big fire and roast the fish we'd caught for dinner. It smelled so delicious and tasted heavenly. Mom would always bring along her signature biscuits and blackberry jam for dessert.

At night I liked to sleep directly under the stars in a sleeping bag. This was a very special time for me. I'd crawl into my sleeping bag and take out a flashlight and my comic books so I could read about my favorite science fiction superhero, Buck Rogers. In the comic series, Buck was a young man who had fallen asleep from radioactive gases in the 20th century. When he woke up 500 years later, Buck and his buddies, Wilma, Buddy, Alura, and Dr. Huer, often found themselves fighting evil invaders from Mars throughout their many futuristic, space-age adventures.

As I drifted off to sleep, images of ray guns, rebel robots, jet packs, radiophones, satellites, rockets, flying saucers, spider-ships, and the Land of the Golden People flooded my mind.

A SWASHBUCKLING SPACE HERO

In 1929, superhero Buck Rogers hit the spotlight in the highly popular newspaper comic strip *Buck Rogers in the 25th Century.* Created by author Philip Francis Nowlan, the fictional Buck Rogers character was depicted as a former US Air Service support pilot stationed in France during World War I. After returning to the United States from Europe, Buck became trapped in a Pennsylvania coal mine where he fell asleep from bizarre radioactive gases. When the young man awakened, it was nearly 500 years later. Buck was immediately thrust into a whole new world of ray guns and evil space people about to take over Earth. Along with his newfound friend, Wilma Deering, Buck ventured to futuristic cities where citizens traveled around in flying saucers and jet packs, ate synthetic food, and used space-age gadgets as everyday tools.

The *Buck Rogers in the 25th Century* comic strip was later featured in radio, television, and motion picture shows, and is credited with bringing the concept of space exploration into popular culture. Tarzan, Popeye, and Tintin were three other comic strip superstars who also debuted in 1929.

2

Barnstormers, Flying Machines, and UFOs

"The desire to fly is an idea handed down to us by our ancestors who, in their grueling travels across trackless lands in prehistoric times, looked enviously on the birds soaring through space, at full speed, above all obstacles, on the infinite highway of the air."

—Wilbur Wright

I was only four years old when I had my first ride on an airplane. Dad and I were walking through a cotton field he sharecropped with my great aunt in Texas, when we spotted a plane in the sky one afternoon. The plane was a Curtiss JN-4 "Jenny" biplane that had two sets of wings built one on top of the other. Because it was so unusual to see aircraft at this time, we couldn't take our eyes off the plane.

But suddenly, to our amazement and alarm, we watched as the plane began to take a serious nosedive. It even looked as if it might crash.

Somehow, the pilot straightened out the plane and managed to land it on a makeshift runway among our rows of white fluffy cotton plants. Dad grabbed my hand and we ran toward the plane to see if the pilot was okay. The young man looked a little shaken but was grinning from ear to ear. He told us he was a barnstormer and had run out of gas, and he apologized for having to make an unfortunate but necessary pit stop on our farm.

Barnstormer was the term for daredevil stunt pilots who performed all sorts of tricks and maneuvers with their planes. Barnstormers were a rare breed of entertainers in America, and many of them had been combat pilots during World War I. These pilots came up with creative ways to earn cash by performing aerial stunts at local flying fields and circuses, or giving people plane rides for a few bucks here and a few bucks there.

Barnstormers seemed to be a fearless bunch of aviators who could do nearly any feat with their planes. They could fly a plane upside down, do a big loop-the-loop in the air, turn a barrel roll in the sky, or even walk on the wing of a plane. It was risky, high-stakes entertainment that was sometimes deadly.

To lend our cotton field barnstormer a hand, Dad drove into town and bought some gas for the pilot so he could refuel. As a way to thank us, the man offered us an exciting ride around the field. The three of us climbed into the two-seat plane, and as I sat on Dad's lap I could feel his strong arms wrap around me, holding me tightly.

As we roared down the cotton field, my stomach swirled and I felt the rush of excitement as the plane lifted up, up into the sky. I felt a little nervous until I looked out the window and saw my world from a whole new perspective. I could see our cotton fields that now looked like big squares of white snow. I could see the clay-colored earth dotted with scrub brush, the tops of trees, and a few tiny-looking horses and cows. It was fantastic.

The 1920s and 1930s were often referred to as the Golden Age of Aviation, and the wild and woolly barnstormers helped American civilians learn to accept and even come to love aviation. But for me, my first ride in a barnstormer's plane planted an important seed in my mind—flying was incredibly fun.

WWII in my Kitchen

I was nine years old when World War II began in 1939. We didn't have a television to show us what was happening during the war, but there were plenty of articles and photographs in newspapers, magazines, and radio stories to paint a vivid picture in my mind.

My dad and uncles were of draft age and could have been required to fight. But because they were farmers, cattle ranchers, and food producers, they were not subject to the draft. Basically they were told to "stay home and produce food for our country and not go to war."

Although Roswell was basically a small farming town, strangely enough, it was also a key military hub for World War II. Two years after the war started, Walker Air Force Base opened in Roswell as a military flying school. I remember looking up at the skies over our ranch and seeing warplanes flying in formation or in training patterns. It was mind-boggling. One minute I'd be riding a horse; the next minute I'd be watching a bomber fly by.

World War II planes fascinated me, and I liked the Pursuit airplanes like the P-51 Mustang, the P-39 Airacobra, or the P-40 Warhawk. Fortunately, companies started to sell aircraft model-making kits that featured these planes. So, on many days after school and when my chores were done, I began to put together wooden model airplanes at the kitchen table. The models came in a small box and all the parts were made of a light balsa wood. Once I'd studied the detailed plans and instructions, I'd carefully put the planes together with glue and then use a small brush to paint them.

Over the years I made all sorts of models like the Curtiss Fighter, the Curtiss Falcon, the Fokker Triplane, or the Boeing Bomber, to name just a few. I'd then fly the ones I could, or I'd hang them with fishing line from my bedroom ceiling.

Flying Solo

In 1944 when I was 14 and about to start high school, my dad decided to move our family to a town called Artesia. He wanted us to be closer to the farm machinery dealership he'd opened there, and closer to the ranch we owned in nearby Hagerman.

Once I started at Artesia High School, I met a lot of new classmates as well as my lifelong friend, Tommy Brown. Tommy and I had many great times together, from shooting basketball hoops to riding on his Cushman motor scooter. He and I would ride all over Artesia and the surrounding towns, and it was a great way to get around.

One day we decided we wanted to get jobs and earn some extra spending money. We took his scooter and rode over to the Artesia Municipal Airport, and straight to the maintenance hangars. We quickly got jobs as flight line boys; we were hired to haul out buckets of hot, soapy water and clean the soot, grime, grease, and bugs from the airplanes. Our pay wasn't in cash; we earned 30 minutes of flight time for our hard work.

Whenever we could, Tommy and I would ride out to the airport to wash planes. Sometimes we'd also fill up the planes' gas tanks, check the oil, or check the tires for air pressure. The time raced by and it didn't even feel like work.

About a year later I had stacked up so many flight hours, I decided to use the earnings to learn how to fly. A flight instructor named Herm agreed to teach me, and I began my flying lessons in a single-wing, two-seat, bright yellow Piper J-3 Cub prop plane. The plane's tandem seating, one seat in front of the other, allowed Herm to sit in the back and guide me as I sat in the front with my own instrument panel and control stick.

At first I learned about the plane and the dials and gauges on the instrument panel so I knew what buttons to switch or knobs to control. I was taught how to move the control stick forward or back to control the elevators on the tail, which moved the plane up or down. I learned how to move the control stick from side to side to control the ailerons on the wings so the plane could turn right, left, or fly in a circle. I was so eager to learn, I would listen intently and focus on everything Herm told me as we flew the plane together. "Keep the wings absolutely level unless you're turning," he'd always say.

Starting the plane was interesting. After Herm turned on a switch in the cockpit, he would walk to the front of the plane and manually spin the propeller about three times to start it. He'd jump into his seat, fasten his seatbelt, and we'd taxi down the runway so I could get a feel for how the plane moved along. We'd then take off and fly in small loops above the ranches and farms before practicing landings. We did this over and over again for the next few weeks until I felt comfortable and confident with the plane. One morning after we'd flown for a while, Herm turned to me with a discernible twinkle in his eye and said, "Okay, Ed—I think you're ready to give it a go." I wasn't sure whether he was serious or not, but I felt like I was ready for my first solo.

"Sure," I said. "Now's a good time as any."

The two of us pulled over alongside the runway, and Herm climbed out. "Take her around and come back. I'll be waiting right here."

"Right," I said, trying to sound as brave as I could.

I tightened my seatbelt and looked over the controls to make sure everything was set correctly. Then I started rolling down the runway going a little bit faster and a little bit faster. I could feel my heart start to pound. I felt somewhat nervous, so I slowed down the plane and temporarily stopped to collect my thoughts. *What if something goes wrong up there? Can I bail out if I need to? What if I crash?*

I turned around to look for Herm, and there he was standing in the same place, smiling and waving me on. I nodded to Herm and remembered what Grandpa Bull used to say, "Steady as she goes, Edgar. Steady as she goes." So I looked straight ahead and started moving the plane down the runway again, going faster and faster. And then, just as Herm taught me, I pulled back on the control stick, and up, up I went.

My heart was still pounding, but this time I was actually flying by myself. My confidence soared as I looped the Piper around and then headed back to land just as I was supposed to. When I finally set the Piper down, Herm was waving his arms and giving me a hearty thumbs-up. It was a great day.

I continued to wash planes and fly as much as I could that year. I knew the landscape and terrain of the Pecos Valley from riding a horse, but now I could see so many amazing sights from above. I saw miles and miles of landscape and waterways. I saw the Capitan Mountains to the west, and the Great Plains and farmland over to the east. I could look down at the large Rio Grande River and the Pecos River where I liked to fish. As I flew over my family's ranches and farms, I was eventually able to pinpoint specific places like my home, Tommy's home, our ranch, and Artesia High School.

A few times I landed my plane on our fields at Hagerman ranch, but Dad was pretty mad about it because it scared the cattle. "Take your flying elsewhere, Edgar," Dad said. And I did.

I remembered the acrobatics of the barnstormer who landed in our cotton field years ago. That now seemed like fun to me, so over time as my flying skills improved, I learned how to do things with my plane like spinning, barrel rolls, and stalling. It was just so exciting and I never felt afraid.

My parents were happy I'd learned to fly because they knew I was the type of kid who was curious, into everything, and always wanting to do more.

And by the time I was 16 I was a fully licensed pilot.

From Atomic Bombs to ETs

Growing up in the Pecos Valley was a kid's paradise of natural springs, rose-colored deserts, and surreal, limestone-laced caverns. It was also an eerie world of strange science, atomic bombs, and talk of mysterious UFO crashes and extraterrestrials.

Only about 5,000 to 6,000 people lived in Roswell when I grew up there, but it always seemed like there was a lot of unusual stuff going on that I heard about either directly or indirectly.

In the fourth and fifth grade, for example, I used to walk about a mile to school on a white gravel road along our farm fields. On most days, I would walk right past the white, two-story home of an elderly man named Dr. Robert Goddard. Sometimes I felt uncomfortable walking by myself because the home was isolated and basically out in the middle of nowhere. I was also a little nervous because some of the townsfolk claimed Goddard was a mad scientist.

Years later I learned that the man was an eminent rocket scientist and considered the father of modern rocketry and space flight in the United States. Little did I know that one day I'd be thankful for the inventions of "crazy" Goddard because his creative and scientific work helped me fly to the Moon.

Very eerie things also happened in the skies around the Roswell area and beyond. One time after I'd gone to bed, I remember looking out my window and seeing a bright flash in the sky that seemed to come up near the distant Capitan Mountains. The flash could be seen for miles and miles and I remember it so vividly.

My parents later explained that the bright light was from the test of the world's first atomic bomb that was being exploded at the Trinity Site of the White Sands Proving Grounds located many miles from our home in New Mexico. We weren't sure what to make of this because it was all so new, and we didn't know the potential danger of nuclear weaponry. But some people say this test in New Mexico ushered in the Atomic Age.

The Roswell Incident

In the summer of 1947 when I was 17 and getting ready to go to college, something happened near Roswell that changed the town, and perhaps my life, forever.

On July 8, 1947, the local paper, the *Roswell Daily Record*, came out with a headline that shook up the entire town. In bold type, the headline read: RAAF CAPTURES FLYING SAUCER ON RANCH IN ROSWELL REGION. RAAF stood for the Roswell Army Air Force.

Like most teenagers, I was naturally curious about the whole thing and wanted to know all about it. Tons of questions raced through my mind. *Was it an alien spacecraft? If so, were the extraterrestrials (ETs) friendly? What would the ETs look like? If there were ETs on the crashed craft, what happened to them?*

Tommy and I thought about taking his scooter out to the ranch where the saucer had supposedly crashed. But we figured it was about 100 miles northwest from where we lived and decided it was too far away. We listened all day to the radio for updates, but not much was reported. I asked my parents about it, but they didn't know much either.

The next day the newspaper came out with a second story
about the incident, saying the UFO was not an alien spacecraft
but was a weather balloon that had crashed on the rancher's
property. Suddenly the whole thing seemed pretty silly, and I
didn't pay much more attention to it at the time. My thoughts
were primarily focused on getting ready to start college at the
Carnegie Institute of Technology in Pennsylvania.

In only 17 years, so much had already happened in my life.
But now it was time to leave home and set out on my own.

ROCKET MAN

Blasting a human into space from the Earth to the Moon
was no easy feat. Thankfully, Dr. Robert Hutchings Goddard, an American physicist and highly gifted inventor,
helped make it happen. He saw the great potential of
future space travel, and his many advances in science
have been crucial for modern day spaceflight.

Goddard was born in 1882 in Worchester, Massachusetts, and is considered by many to be the "father of
modern rocketry." As a teenager, he climbed into a tree
and had an "aha" moment that redirected his lifework.
He suddenly imagined how fantastic it would be to be
able to fly into space—even to Mars!

Robert Goddard grew up during the advent of electric power. Although he suffered from tuberculosis as a
child and missed a great deal of school, he was an avid
reader and had a strong interest in science. One of his

favorite books was H. G. Wells's science fiction novel, *The War of the Worlds.*

He went on to build the world's first liquid-fueled rocket, which he successfully launched on March 16, 1926, in Auburn, Massachusetts. But his revolutionary research and wild ideas of flying into space were often ridiculed, especially in mainstream media. As a result, Goddard became reclusive and eventually moved to Roswell, New Mexico, in 1930. There he found wide-open spaces to build, test, and launch his rockets.

Dr. Robert Goddard's pioneering work in rocketry was recognized and honored after his death in 1945. In 1959, the US Congress honored Goddard as the "Father of Space Flight." That same year, the National Aeronautics and Space Administration (NASA) chose the name Goddard Space Flight Center for its first space flight complex.

3

Spreading My Wings

> "The most difficult thing is the decision to act, the rest is merely tenacity. The fears are paper tigers. You can do anything you decide to do. You can act to change and control your life; and the procedure, the process is its own reward."
>
> —Amelia Earhart

The day I left home to head off to college, Mom, Dad, Sandra, Jay, Tommy, and many of my relatives came to the train station to say good-bye. I was excited to be going to Carnegie Tech in Pittsburgh, Pennsylvania, but it was hard to think about leaving behind everything I'd known.

Mom handed me a sack lunch to take on my trip and gave me a big hug. When the train whistle blew, I knew it was time to go. I boarded the train and quickly grabbed a window seat so I could lean out and wave good-bye to everyone. As Sandra and Jay waved back, I could see this wasn't easy for them and I knew we'd miss each other.

Shortly after the train moved out of the station, I opened up my sack lunch and polished off my favorite sandwich, a burger with cheese, which Mom had made me. I then settled in for the long 1,500-mile journey winding through New Mexico, Oklahoma, Illinois, Indiana, Ohio, and then on over to Pennsylvania. As I looked out at the beautiful fields and farmlands that I'd either worked or played on as a child, I wondered if the train was traveling over the very tracks Grandpa Mitchell and my dad had laid down so many years ago. And as the train methodically chugged along through the many small towns and a big city here or there, I tried to imagine the new world that was awaiting me.

Choosing Carnegie

Although Carnegie Tech was a long way from home, the decision to go there was a good one. I had thought long and hard about my college choices during my senior year at Artesia High School. At one point I even considered going to school to study music.

But my math and science teacher, Robert Parham, encouraged me to apply to more technical, science-based schools like Carnegie Mellon, the Massachusetts Institute of Technology (MIT), and the California Institute of Technology (Caltech). Mr. Parham helped me fill out all my applications, and he was a wonderful role model and great mentor in my life. I felt very appreciative of his help.

Carnegie Tech, which is now called Carnegie Mellon, was the first school to accept me as a college student, and I thought this was a good sign of where I should go. My parents also had friends who lived in the Pittsburgh area, so there was a strong family connection for me.

But when I finally got to my freshman dorm, I suddenly felt apprehensive about everything. I wondered if my professors and classmates would think I was some just some straw-headed cowboy from the farm. Then I quickly realized that most of the new kids I met had similar feelings about fitting in.

After I hung up my clothes and made up my bed, I headed outside to check out the campus. I first walked to the Hunt Library that was located in the quad area called "The Cut." I noticed that instead of the traditional red brick buildings that are so common in eastern universities, Carnegie had sandy colored brick buildings with green roofs. There were also a lot of trees and grass, and coming from the dry, arid Southwest, I liked what I saw. Plus, I was really looking forward to being outside in the winter snow.

During my freshman year, I enjoyed classes in basic subjects such as chemistry, calculus, history, and the language arts. Sometimes on the weekends I'd take a bus or streetcar to visit my parents' friends and have dinner. And every once in a while I would babysit their young daughter, which was a nice diversion from my studies.

In my sophomore year I had a full course schedule and I also joined the Kappa Sigma fraternity. I was busy, there was a lot to do, and I had expenses to cover. So to earn a little extra spending money, a fraternity brother and I took part-time jobs at the Bethlehem Steel Mills near Pittsburgh. We worked nights cleaning blast furnaces, and we'd go back to Carnegie Tech and get up the next day to go to class. It was hot, dirty, and exhausting work, but it paid pretty well.

One day, some of my buddies and I had taken a trolley car to go into Pittsburgh to do some shopping. At the back of the trolley, there was a pretty girl with dark brown hair and a big smile standing with a few other girls. I managed to strike up a conversation with her and found out that her name was Louise Randall, and she was studying painting and design at Carnegie.

Louise and I started to have meals together at the Skibo cafeteria on campus, and before long we were dating. A few years later Louise and I got married on December 21, 1951, in her hometown of Mount Lebanon, Pennsylvania. We honeymooned in New York City.

The following spring we both attended our graduation ceremony; Louise earned a degree in art and I earned a degree in industrial management. It felt great to be getting on with my life, and being with Louise was wonderful. Planning out the next part of our lives came next. Grandpa Mitchell wasn't feeling well, so it made sense for me to return to New Mexico to work in our Artesia farm machinery dealership and manage the Hagerman ranch. Louise and I said good-bye to our Carnegie friends and Louise's family, and piled everything we owned into my green Ford coupe to drive cross-country to New Mexico. I wondered how Louise was going to like living in the Southwest because it was so different from the East Coast. But she seemed eager to go, and that made me happy.

The Zigzag Years

After I began my new work at the dealership and Hagerman ranch, we moved into one of my great aunt's houses in Artesia. Louise had just started to decorate the home and make it our own when I got some surprising news that neither of us liked.

The Korean War was on, and I was about to be drafted into the war. I really didn't want to be drafted, so I decided it would be best if I enlisted. And I knew that if I were going to be in the military, I wanted to fly. I immediately enlisted in the navy because the air force had more restrictions for married men at the time.

Enlisting in the navy became a key decision and turning point for my entire career. It wasn't what I was expecting to do with my life, but that's what happened. Suddenly, our new "military life" set Louise and me on a tremendously hectic journey that zigzagged us to many different towns all across the United States for many years.

Our very first move was to San Diego, California, where I began basic training, also known as boot camp, at the Naval Training Center. Louise followed shortly thereafter and took a job in a restaurant waiting tables while living in a nearby motel. I was required to live on the military base, and it wasn't a whole heck of a lot of fun with our separate accommodations. But it was nice to be in San Diego near the water, and on the weekends we'd often go to the ocean to swim and just relax on the beach.

After basic training, which lasted about six weeks, I was assigned to begin Officer Candidate School (OCS) in Newport, Rhode Island. Louise and I loaded up the Ford coupe and headed east, across the country once again.

When we got to Newport, Louise and I were shocked when we realized we'd gone through nearly all our money. We were hungry, but I only had about 25 cents in my pocket.

So, to tide us over, we split a hot dog and a cup of coffee. I then raced over to the OCS naval station to report to duty and pick up my first paycheck. Thankfully, we had enough money to go out for a nicer meal.

After less than six months in Rhode Island, I had become an ensign in the navy and Louise had become pregnant with our first child. It was 1953 and also time to move on again.

Our next destination was Pensacola, Florida. We packed up our trusty car and drove to Pennsylvania to visit Louise's parents before jumping onto Interstate 95 and heading south to Florida. On the long, hot drive we'd roll down the windows and turn on the radio to listen to some of our favorite singers like Johnny Cash, Ella Fitzgerald, and Elvis Presley, who were chart toppers at the time. It was fun looking out the window because the South had a distinct look compared to other places I'd lived. We passed by many fragrant orange and grapefruit groves, and I'll never forget seeing the strange-looking Spanish moss hanging from some of the trees.

Once we arrived in Pensacola, we wound up renting a house near the naval base. But homes weren't easy to come by because there were a lot of young military couples looking to rent.

Louise and I realized that if we wanted to find a home, we needed to beat the crowd. The two of us would wake up early and drive to the local newspaper office to get the papers that were hot off the press so we could check out the newest homes advertised in the classifieds. The idea worked. One morning we found an address we both liked and parked our car in front of the place until it was a respectable hour to knock on the door. We talked with the owners and eventually got the home.

Later that year, our first daughter, Karlyn, was born. As Louise stayed home and was busy taking care of Karlyn, I was at the base, busy learning how to fly the North American AT-6/SNJ Texan, which was the navy's basic aircraft trainer. But we weren't in Florida very long.

After learning to fly the AT-6, I was then required to have more advanced flight training. So, once again, we packed up and moved our small family to yet another location. This time it was to the Hutchinson Naval Air Station in Hutchinson, Kansas, where I learned how to fly P2V Maritime patrol planes like the "Neptune."

In just a short time, my life had changed dramatically from studying at Carnegie and working on our ranches. I'd prepared to be a naval officer and a skilled navy pilot, and I'd moved my family from California to Rhode Island, and from Florida to Kansas.

Our next move was to the Pacific Northwest, where I was finally stationed at the naval air station on foggy but lush Whidbey Island in Washington State. This is where Louise and I bought our first home, and we had happy visions of settling down.

And then it was time to go to war.

Risky Pacific Skies

My first navy deployment was to the island of Okinawa, Japan, for a six-month tour of duty with a patrol squadron. I was only 24 at the time and it was a big, big change. Even though I'd visited the San Francisco World's Fair when I was nine, toured Washington, DC, with my grandmother when

I was a teen, and lived in nearly 10 towns across the United States throughout my life, Japan was a very different environment and it took time to adjust. I was overseas in a foreign land where I didn't speak the language, and I felt like I was a million miles away from home. I tried to stay connected with Louise and Karlyn through letters and international phone calls, but I missed them a great deal.

As a naval aviator, my duties were to fly the P2V Neptune with a four-man crew (pilot, copilot, crew chief, and gunner) to patrol the Pacific along the coastal waters of Japan, China, and Korea. It was an extremely tense, risky time, and I quickly discovered how dangerous and deadly war could be.

I came close to losing my life on the last day of a six-month tour of duty when I was getting ready to fly home to be with my family. I was flying on routine night duty, patrolling the waters and watching the ships going in and out around the straits near Shanghai, China. Suddenly my radar showed two attack jets rapidly approaching. Without a second thought, I immediately and instinctively thrust my controls forward, sending my plane into a sharp nosedive. It was lucky I did this because I watched incandescent tracer bullets from one of the attack jets whiz right over me!

After I got back to the base, I had to describe what happened during the attack. First I had to write a full report about the attack, and then I was interrogated by management, who asked me about all the details. I was so exhausted after all of this that I crawled into one of our airplanes that was heading home and immediately fell asleep.

But the good news was that I was finally flying home.

From Prop Planes to Jets

After I got back to Whidbey Island and was looking forward to a bit of downtime with Louise and Karlyn, we were immediately transferred to San Diego.

I was now assigned to carrier duty to fly faster A-3 Skywarrior jets that took off and landed from enormous aircraft carriers. The ships were huge floating airbases where there wasn't much room for error; a pilot had to have a good sense of judgment and skill to get the plane on and off the water-based runway fast and accurately. But flying jets was thrilling. I was always drawn to the cutting edge of flight technology, and jets were a new kind of speedier aircraft that was very exciting to fly.

While living in San Diego, I flew for three years in the Pacific during the Korean conflict and the Cold War, and I had two deployments to the Pacific waters near Japan. The first deployment was on the USS *Bonhomme Richard* aircraft carrier, and the second was on the USS *Ticonderoga* aircraft carrier.

Over time the navy realized I was a highly skilled pilot, so I was assigned to test pilot duty, which was something entirely new. This new assignment meant moving my family yet again to a place in California called China Lake.

China Lake was a very isolated and barren town near the Mojave Desert. Here, my duties were to figure out how to fly planes to drop bombs below enemy radar and then speed away.

And then in the fall of 1957, when I was 27 years old, something changed my life for good. I was returning to the States from being overseas and I heard about something extraordinary that happened in the skies above Earth.

And it was shocking news.

4

NASA Here We Come

> *"This above all: to thine own self be true."*
>
> —William Shakespeare

On October 4, 1957, I was aboard the USS *Ticonderoga* aircraft carrier and traveling home from my latest assignment in the Pacific. I was en route to our newest home in China Lake, and I'm sure Louise and Karlyn were eagerly awaiting my return. But like so many people around the world on this day, I had the radio turned on and my attention turned toward the heavens. The announcer sounded intense as he reported that the Russians had just launched *Sputnik 1*, the very first manmade satellite, into Earth's orbit.

The news about *Sputnik* spread rapidly and shocked a lot of people, including me, because the Russians had kept information about the spacecraft top secret until the day of the launch. I wanted to know all about this round, mysterious craft. In Russian, the word *Sputnik* means "fellow traveler of the

Earth." The satellite was a round metallic object about twice the size of a basketball. It weighed 184 pounds, traveled about 18,000 miles per hour, and was located about 139 miles above Earth at its closest point.

The launch of *Sputnik* was a huge world event and immediately covered by the media. The *New York Times* headline read: SOVIET FIRES EARTH SATELLITE INTO SPACE; IT IS CIRCULING THE GLOBE AT 18,000 MPH.; SPHERE TRACKED IN 4 CROSSINGS OVER US.

The Russians then launched a second *Sputnik* one month later on November 3, 1957. This satellite was bigger than *Sputnik 1* and had a dog aboard named Pupnik Laika. The dog was an even-tempered little terrier and the first living creature to travel in "outer" space. I couldn't help but think about my childhood terrier, Oscar. Unfortunately, Laika died within hours of *Sputnik 2*'s launch.

I suddenly realized that outer space was a new frontier for human exploration, and I just knew that human beings would follow right behind robotic satellites and animals in space. There's no other way to say it—*Sputnik* changed my life. I wanted to be a part of this exciting new field, and I was absolutely sure that I wanted to be a space explorer. But in order to do this I also realized I needed to go back to college and get more education.

My mind was bursting with ideas, and I couldn't wait to tell Louise all about them. I'd also been thinking a lot about being in the military. When I was a boy, I thought that war and fighting were natural things humans did for the greater good. But after facing near-death situations and seeing so much death and destruction, I became turned off to war. I wanted to use my skills as a pilot in nonviolent ways. I realized that becoming an astronaut would launch me in a whole new direction on a whole new peaceful path.

I just had to figure out how to get there.

From China Lake to Carmel

While we were still living in China Lake, Louise gave birth to our second daughter and we named her Elizabeth. We were all so happy to welcome Elizabeth, and I remember Karlyn was delighted to have a baby sister. Our young family was growing and our lives were changing.

With my mind set on going back to college, I started to investigate graduate-level programs offered by the navy. One option available to me was at the US Naval Postgraduate School in Monterey, California, where I could study the emerging field of aeronautics. In 1959, I decided that a move to Monterey, which is by the ocean, would be one my family would like. Elizabeth was nearly one, Karlyn was six, and Louise was eager to get out of isolated China Lake.

So we headed west from the California desert to the California coastline and found a new home in Carmel Valley. Carmel was a beautiful change of scenery with its white sandy beaches, rolling hills, cypress trees, and vineyards.

After I was accepted into the Naval Postgraduate School, I began to study more technical subjects in aeronautics. I learned a lot about aircraft, aircraft engines, and flight profiles, and it was a great change to get out of the seat of a warplane and into the seat of a classroom. Most important, I was sticking to my plan to become an astronaut.

Recruiting All Astronauts

When *Sputnik* was launched in 1957, Dwight D. Eisenhower was president of the United States. Some of our leaders didn't like the fact the Russians had been first in space; they were worried that a satellite like *Sputnik* might have the potential to carry something like a nuclear weapon. People quickly realized that the space around our planet could become a kind of invisible war zone where high-altitude battles might be waged.

Although the United States and the Soviet Union (USSR) had fought together as allies to end World War II, there was still a great deal of discord between the two countries. Distrust was rampant because both countries possessed nuclear weapons, which had enormous destructive potential worldwide.

It didn't take long before a new war, called the Cold War, began. This war was deemed "cold" because there was no direct military action, but there was an enormous amount of hostility and suspicion. During this era, which occurred in the late 1950s and early 1960s, children in America were taught to "duck and cover" under school desks in the event of a nuclear bomb. Some families built underground bomb shelters in their backyards. World War II and the Korean War were over, but there was still a great deal of conflict and fear.

On top of this, the Russians and Americas started to take sides in what was called the "space race," a celestial competition to see which country would achieve more progress in space. The race was on to see who would have the best spacecraft; who would fly the fastest, highest, and farthest; and who would be top dog in this new frontier.

I paid close attention to nearly everything that was happening in the growing field of astronautics. President Eisenhower wanted America to forge ahead in space exploration and he helped form NASA, the National Aeronautics and Space Administration. NASA was founded on October 1, 1958, to conduct civilian research for space flight.

President Eisenhower also asked universities such as MIT, Caltech, and Princeton to set up graduate programs in space science, aeronautics, and astronautics because, frankly, nobody knew what was "out there" in deep space.

Space Age Studies

"The most beautiful experience we can have is the mysterious." —Albert Einstein

After earning my bachelor of science in aeronautics from the Naval Postgraduate School in 1961, I was one of the first students to be accepted into the new astronautics program at MIT in Cambridge, Massachusetts. I was still an officer in the navy and would now focus my studies on advances in aeronautics and astronautics, and thought-provoking courses in physics and quantum mechanics.

It wasn't easy moving from Carmel Valley to Cambridge, but a new home near Boston had many advantages. Sometimes my family went to Boston to shop or see a museum, we took summer vacations in Cape Cod, and the girls liked playing outside in the snow and ice skating. Louise was wonderful about all our moves to different towns every few years, but there's no question it was tough on her. When we got married we hadn't planned our lives around going off to war and having such a nomadic lifestyle. Heading to MIT was a bit of a reprieve, because we were going to stay put in Cambridge for the three years it took to get my degree.

Because the astronautics program at MIT was in its infancy, new curriculum about space needed to be developed. I took interesting courses in subjects such as the evolution of the universe and star systems, space guidance and navigation, spacecraft control systems, and rocket propulsion. I also started to learn about computer programming, which was in its infancy in the early 1960s. It was obvious that computers would be incredibly important in space.

Student discussions, sometimes exhilarating, sometimes argumentative, revolved on cosmic questions about the what-ifs and whys of the universe. I started to wonder about the cosmos more than ever and realized there were many unanswered questions. It was cerebral, fun, and fascinating stuff to consider. But I also knew there was a lot of fear and confusion. I remember hearing about Orson Welles's *The War of the Worlds* radio broadcast that aired in 1938 when I was eight years old. The radio show pretended to be an actual newscast about an extraterrestrial invasion, and some folks thought it was real and became frightened. I also thought about the alleged UFO crash that happened in Roswell when I was 17— and the great stir it caused.

Ten Years to the Moon

I was at MIT in 1961 when John F. Kennedy became president of the United States after Eisenhower left office. In that year, President Kennedy announced to Congress the ambitious, 10-year goal of having an American astronaut land on the Moon and safely return to Earth before the end of the decade.

Ten years to the Moon? I took it as a personal challenge. I wanted to go to the Moon.

The following is an excerpt from John F. Kennedy's famous speech, "The Decision to Go to the Moon," which was delivered before a joint session of Congress on May 25, 1961.

First, I believe that this nation should commit itself to achieving the goal, before this decade is out, of landing a man on the Moon and returning him safely to the Earth. No single space project in this period will be more impressive to mankind, or more important for the long-range exploration of space; and none will be so difficult or expensive to accomplish. We propose to accelerate the development of the appropriate lunar spacecraft. We propose to develop alternate liquid and solid fuel boosters, much larger than any now being developed, until certain, which is superior. We propose additional funds for other engine development and for unmanned exploration—explorations, which are particularly important for one purpose which this nation will never overlook . . . the survival of the man who first makes this daring flight.

—John F. Kennedy, May 25, 1961

A Big Disappointment

Although I enjoyed studying at MIT, I was very glad to graduate. My doctoral thesis was titled "Guidance of Low-Thrust Interplanetary Vehicles," and I earned my doctor of science (Sc.D) in 1964. Other future astronauts, such as Buzz Aldrin, Dave Scott, and Charlie Duke, were also studying and getting their degrees from MIT during the years when I was there.

After graduation I was raring to go, but not exactly sure what to do. I eventually applied for a position in the guidance control division of NASA located in Houston, Texas, and was accepted. Houston was definitely the place to be if you wanted to be an astronaut.

Louise, the kids, and I knew the drill. We packed up the car and started driving west toward Texas. Finally my dream to become an astronaut was really coming true. At least for a few hours.

On our drive, we stopped at Louise's mother's home in Pennsylvania. That's when I got a phone call from Navy Captain Jack Van Ness, who delivered some very disappointing news. Jack informed me the navy wanted me to work on a new project in Los Angeles called the Manned Orbiting Laboratory, which would be part of the military's space surveillance program.

So, although I had my heart set on Houston, we headed to Los Angeles.

For nearly a year and a half I worked on the Manned Orbiting Laboratory and oversaw many people who helped design this state-of-the-art spacecraft. But once it became clear to me that the orbiting lab project was starting to stall, I realized this job wasn't going to help me get to the Moon. To get to the Moon, I needed a lot more time flying newer and faster jets. I remembered good advice I'd heard throughout my life: "If at first you don't succeed, try, try again." So I tried again.

A Great Move

I knew Edwards Air Force Base wasn't that far from L.A. and had an Aerospace Research Pilot School headed by the legendary test pilot Chuck Yeager. Jack Van Ness understood my aspirations to walk on the Moon, so I asked him if he could help get me assigned to the school. Thankfully, he did just that.

In 1965, my next big adventure was learning to fly exotic supersonic jets at Edwards Air Force Base, which was located in the middle of the Mojave Desert. During the week I would say good-bye to Louise and the girls, who were happy to stay in Los Angeles, and I'd fly up to Edwards. I'd then return to be with my family on the weekends.

Edwards Air Force Base was an exciting place to be with an amazing agenda of flight programs. It was certainly a dynamic time in my life. Suddenly I was flying planes faster and higher than I ever had in my life, and I even flew high-performance, supersonic aircraft such as the Lockheed NF-104 that could reach altitudes of more than 100,000 feet.

At Edwards, I was both a student and an instructor in the school's new space-training program. I taught a wide range of subjects such as advanced mathematics, navigation theory, aviation, astronomy, and orbital mechanics to budding astronauts.

Then one spring evening in 1966, I was back in Los Angeles having dinner with my family. The phone rang and it was astronaut Deke Slayton on the line. Deke was NASA's coordinator of astronaut activities and worked in Houston at the Manned Spacecraft Center, which was named the Johnson Space Center in 1973. It seemed like I'd been waiting years for a call from him.

Deke said he'd like me to move to Houston and begin astronaut training. I immediately said yes! I was 36 years old at the time, and all my hard work and willingness to be flexible had paid off.

After I hung up the phone, I swooped up Louise and the girls in a big family hug.

5

Getting There

> "The journey of a thousand miles begins with the first step."
>
> —Lao-tzu

After so many years of hard work I had finally landed at NASA, and it felt great to be part of the Apollo team. In 1966 I was chosen along with 18 other men to participate in NASA's Group 5 astronaut training. We were all test pilots and we all had college degrees.

Every day at the Manned Spacecraft Center there was a tremendous feeling that all our work was going to make history. And it certainly did. I also felt that going to the Moon was a big step in the advancement of our species, and I was honored to be a part of it.

After arriving in Houston I immediately started ground school. All of the Group 5 astronauts took refresher courses in math and physics and learned about subjects such as space science, astronomy, geology, orbital mechanics, computer science, space flight, and the medical aspects of space flight. We also learned about complex spacecraft equipment such as propulsion control systems and fuel cells, and we took courses in how to observe and photograph phenomena in space.

The Apollo Program

Named after the Greek god of light, the Sun, truth, prophecy, and music, the Apollo program's overarching goal was to safely land humans on the Moon and safely return them to Earth.

But exploration of the Moon was not new. In the 17th century, physicist Galileo Galilei was one of the first astronomers to use a telescope to look at the Milky Way galaxy and observe the mountains and craters of the Moon. In 1959, the Soviet Union launched a robotic probe called *Luna 2*, which was the first man-made spacecraft to reach and impact the lunar surface.

Landing a man on the Moon was no easy task. It was the result of decades of space exploration and preparation, and it was a careful and patient process with many valuable lessons learned along the way—even the painful ones.

After *Sputnik 1* was launched in 1957, the United States launched *Explorer 1* in 1958, which was our first man-made satellite. Great advances in space were made in America as well as in Russia during this time.

In the United States, NASA's Project Mercury (the first US human spaceflight program, which ran from 1961 to 1963) proved that one man could orbit the Earth and return safely. Project Gemini (the second US human spaceflight program, which ran from 1965 to 1966) was designed to perfect important rendezvous and docking procedures that would be required for going to the Moon. Project Mercury and Project Gemini helped pave the way for a Moon landing and preceded the Apollo program, which landed men on the Moon from 1969 to 1972.

In 1961, the first humans to travel in space were Russian cosmonaut Yuri Gagarin, followed by American astronauts Alan Shepard and Gus Grissom.

America's many astronauts, scientists, engineers, and physicians worked tirelessly to figure out how to fly humans in space, and how to do it in the best and safest way possible. In total there were 12 manned Apollo lunar missions: 1, 7, 8, 9, 10, 11, 12, 13, 14, 15, 16, and 17. Some of the missions were designed to orbit the Earth, some were designed to orbit the Moon, and some were designed to land men on the Moon. The Apollo lunar missions 11, 12, 14, 15, 16, and 17 landed men on the Moon, and the 12 astronauts who walked on the Moon were:

- Apollo 11
  Launch: July 16, 1969–Landing: July 24, 1969
  Neil Alden Armstrong (Commander)
  Edwin Eugene "Buzz" Aldrin Jr. (Lunar Module Pilot)
- Apollo 12
  Launch: November 14, 1969–Landing: November 24, 1969
  Charles "Pete" Conrad Jr. (Commander)
  Alan LaVern Bean (Lunar Module Pilot)

◗ **Apollo 14**
Launch: January 31, 1971–Landing: February 9, 1971
Alan Bartlett Shepard Jr. (Commander)
Edgar Dean Mitchell, Sc.D (Lunar Module Pilot)

◗ **Apollo 15**
Launch: July 26, 1971–Landing: August 7, 1971
David Randolph Scott (Commander)
James Benson Irwin (Lunar Module Pilot)

◗ **Apollo 16**
Launch: April 16, 1972–Landing: April 27, 1972
John Watts Young (Commander)
Charles "Charlie" Moss Duke Jr. (Lunar Module Pilot)

◗ **Apollo 17**
Launch: December 7, 1972–Landing: December 19, 1972
Eugene "Gene" Andrew Cernan (Commander)
Harrison Hagan "Jack" Schmitt (Lunar Module Pilot)

I was with NASA for six years from 1966 to 1972, and I had six major astronaut assignments:

1969: Apollo 9—Member of the Astronaut Support Crew

1969: Apollo 10—Backup Lunar Module Pilot

1971: Apollo 14—Lunar Module Pilot (The sixth man to walk on the Moon)

1971: Apollo 15—CAPCOM (Lunar Module Landing and Launch)

1972: Apollo 16—Backup Lunar Module Pilot

1972: Apollo 16—CAPCOM (Lunar Extravehicular Activity)

Project #1: Design a Moon Lander

Many of the spacecraft parts and systems for the Apollo program were constructed across the country and around the world, and it was very common to work in different cities other than Houston. My first big project at NASA was at the Grumman Aircraft facility in Bethpage, Long Island, where I helped design and test a state-of-the-art Moon vehicle called a Lunar Module (LM) that was appropriately named *Spider*. Every week I'd fly to Grumman in Long Island with fellow astronaut Fred Haise to work on this unusual spacecraft. I remember the first time Fred and I took a gander at the *Spider*. All we could say was, "Wow—how in the world is that thing supposed to fly us down to the Moon?"

But this bug-like spacecraft worked quite well. It was designed to carry two astronauts away from their main spacecraft, the Command Module, and then fly them to the surface of the Moon. It would then launch and fly the astronauts back up to the Command Module after their lunar work was done so the crew could return to Earth. It would also act as a miniature home where the astronauts would eat, sleep, and prepare for excursions on the surface of the Moon.

With its spindly legs, boxy parts, and shiny metallic covering, the LM looked like an elaborate invention cartoonist Rube Goldberg might have drawn. It was about 23 feet tall and its long legs could fold inward so it could be stored in the Saturn V launch vehicle.

The LM was strictly designed for function so it could land us on the Moon and get us off the Moon with minimum weight. The odd, unglamorous look of the LM wasn't important; it didn't need to be streamlined and aerodynamic because it was going to fly in the Moon's airless, reduced gravity. And since it wasn't going to return to Earth, it only needed to be strong enough to withstand the lunar landing.

The work Fred and I were doing was critical. We needed to make sure that this spacecraft was going to function efficiently and be completely safe on the Moon. We tested it over and over again from the astronaut's point of view so that it was sensible to use and practical to fly. Fred and I checked and rechecked the cabin area for the location of instruments and gauges so that everything was easy to reach. We also had to conduct many tests of the vehicle in an altitude chamber that had zero air pressure.

After the Spider, eight more Lunar Modules were built: *Snoopy, Eagle, Intrepid, Aquarius, Antares, Falcon, Orion,* and *Challenger.*

Training, Training, and More Training

"In order to equip each astronaut with an understanding of space-related problems and the knowledge he will need to solve them, a continuing program of astronaut training activities is conducted." —Deke Slayton, NASA director of flight crew operations, 1968

It took a great deal of study and preparation to fly 240,000 miles to the Moon and then 240,000 back home again. For each mission the Apollo teams rehearsed for many months.

As astronauts in training, we practiced indoors, outdoors, on land, underwater, in the air, and, of course, in the many different devices that simulated the spacecraft we would eventually fly one day. We were launched, dropped, spun, and dunked in a variety of unique conditions. We did all of this ahead of time so we could experience the many sensations, noises, and vibrations of space flight as well figure out how it would feel to work in the weightlessness of space and the reduced gravity of the Moon.

Figuring out how to be prepared and survive in different environments was something I learned when I was a Boy Scout growing up in New Mexico. It's interesting to note that of the 12 men who walked on the Moon, 11 were Boy Scouts. And now I was learning all sorts of new survival skills in preparation for my journey to the Moon. The astronauts had to be fully prepared for so many different tasks—being able to operate different kinds of spacecraft, being able to live and work in the spacecraft, landing on the Moon, working on the Moon, and then flying home. We also needed to know how to calmly handle any kind of problem or crisis we might encounter in space. None of this was taken lightly. It was serious stuff.

Exploring the Moon on Earth

A big part of our training was to figure out what it was going to be like to walk and work on the Moon once we got there. And the best way to learn about this unusual lunar environment was to travel to places around the world that were barren like the Moon and that also had craters.

NASA arranged for us to have geology field trips (GFTs) all over the planet, and I was amazed to learn about the many unusual "moon-like" worlds right here on Earth. From Texas to Iceland, we traveled to enormous craters, barren deserts, canyons, caverns, and areas with volcanic eruptions. On our many GFTs we collected, measured, inspected, documented, and photographed all sorts of igneous, sedimentary, and metamorphic rocks. We were learning a lot about many different kinds of rocks so we could be the "eyes and ears" of geologists when we were on the Moon collecting Moon rocks.

One of my most memorable trips was to the volcanically active and very remote region of central Askja, Iceland, in July 1967. Known for its volcanic craters called calderas, this region had a very rocky terrain with black volcanic sand, as well as a large lake and hot springs. It was a misty, surreal place unlike anything I'd ever seen in my travels. And because we were there during the summer it seemed like the sun never set.

Another one of our major field trips was to the enormous Nördlinger Ries Crater in Bavaria, Germany, in August 1970. This large round depression on Earth was created by the impact of a gigantic meteorite millions of years ago. At Nördlinger Ries we were able to study rock formations that would be similar to those on the Moon also created by meteorite impacts.

We also explored other sites such as the Grand Canyon and the Meteor Crater in Arizona; the Big Bend region of west Texas; Bend, Oregon; Katmai, Alaska; Valles Caldera and Zuni Salt Lake, New Mexico; Pinacates, Mexico; the Big Island of Hawaii; Craters of the Moon in Idaho, and even areas of the Nevada Test Site.

We worked for many months in the field and essentially earned the equivalent of a master's degree in geology in field training. This was a whole new area of study in my life, and I thought it was incredibly intriguing and helpful.

The Vomit Comet and the Torture Chamber

In addition to managing to work and survive in extraterrestrial places, we needed to be able to travel in our high-powered, rocket-based spacecraft. Our bodies needed to be able to withstand unusual G-forces, as with the liftoff of our rocket, or with zero gravity (zero G), which is the reduced gravity of being in space.

To experience the weightlessness of zero G, we either flew in high-speed aircraft or we went underwater. And to experience more than one G (increased gravity), as with liftoff, we'd spin incredibly fast in a centrifuge.

During what's called parabolic training, the astronauts had the opportunity to feel short periods of weightlessness. We were able to do this in what we liked to refer to as the Vomit Comet because some of the guys would feel nauseous and toss their cookies, so to speak. We'd climb aboard a KC-135 aircraft that would shoot us up high in a steep trajectory and then descend rapidly in a free fall so we'd have about 20 to 60 seconds of zero G weightlessness, allowing us to float around the padded cabin. We practiced different maneuvers in the Vomit Comet wearing our space suits, and sometimes we'd take along lunar equipment, like the modularized equipment transporter (MET), to see how lugging this cart would feel in reduced gravity.

We also traveled to the naval base in Warminster, Pennsylvania, for training in the Johnsville centrifuge. We'd reluctantly climb in a steel orb called the Gondola, which was about 10 feet in diameter and suspended at the end of a long metal arm. Once we were buckled in, the device would spin us around and around at a G-force that would simulate rocket liftoff and reentry into the atmosphere. Nobody liked getting into this bizarre device that some of us nicknamed the "wheel," the "torture chamber," or the "gruesome merry-go-round." But it gave us valuable information about how our bodies responded to movement, spinning, and the feeling of a heavy weight pressing against the body as happens during liftoff.

Zero G Under the Sea

Of course, one of the best places an astronaut can feel the weightlessness of zero gravity is underwater, so we were trained as scuba divers at the US Naval School for Underwater Swimmers in Key West, Florida. This training gave us an opportunity to learn how to navigate an aquatic environment; we learned basic principles like how to breathe in a strange environment that has no air, and how to become accustomed to new and unusual environments like the Moon. This training also prepared us for the time our space capsule would reenter Earth's atmosphere and splash down in the ocean.

Braised Boas for Lunch?

It wasn't a sure thing that our Command Module would be able to plummet from space and soar perfectly through Earth's searing atmosphere to splash down at a specific location in the ocean. That was the plan, but in the event our capsule didn't hit its watery target, or that it needed to return to Earth quickly, we needed to be prepared to survive in a variety of remote, hostile environments like the jungle or the desert. So, another important aspect of our work was survival training.

In June 1967, I was part of a small group of astronauts who spent four days in the Panama Jungle Survival School, near the Panama Canal. We first went to a classroom in the jungle where we learned survival basics such as how to build a simple shelter, how to find and prepare food and water, and how to hike and navigate through the dense, rugged rain forest. Part of our classroom lessons included being treated to a "jungle buffet" consisting of foods such as boa, fried rat, iguana, hearts of palm, and taro root.

After this basic instruction, we were dropped off in the jungle via a helicopter, and we grouped ourselves into three-man teams like our Apollo crews. It was our job to scout down a campsite and then build a lean-to using large palm leaves to protect us from the scorching sun and drenching rain. Our only supplies were items such as a first-aid kit and a parachute, which were items we would have with us on our spacecraft during our missions.

For the few days we were on our own, we mostly ate plant-based foods and we intentionally avoided eating things like bugs, frogs, worms, and other creepy crawlers. I remember chopping down a palm tree in extremely hot weather to find the edible inner core, the heart of palm, which most of us did eat.

And then, a few months later during the scorching month of August 1967, I traveled to the desert of Pasco, Washington, for survival training in approximately 110-degree temperatures. Here, along with a small group of astronauts, I spent two days in a classroom learning different survival techniques before spending three long, hot days in the desert. The only items we were allowed to take with us were a survival kit, a parachute, and three-and-a-half quarts of water. The parachute turned out to be very handy on this trip; we draped it around our bodies like a flowing robe to protect our skin from the sun. We also braided strips of the parachute to make a twine, and we used another part of the parachute to make a tent.

Because water is so crucial in the dry desert, we learned how to make a solar still to collect potable water, and how to squeeze moisture from a cactus. There were slim pickins for dinner unless anybody felt like a meal made from snakes, lizards, ants, rabbits, or birds—if you could snare them.

Learning to survive in different regions of the world wasn't easy, but it was essential training so that we could survive no matter where our spacecraft landed us back on Earth. This training was also helpful in teaching us how to cope and adapt to unknown environments.

Spacecraft Simulators

We also had to know ahead of time about every big and small detail that would go right, as well as every little thing that might go wrong.

To learn this, a great deal of our training revolved around rehearsing what we were about to do in space, in exact replicas of our spacecraft. We often worked in Command Module and Lunar Module simulators to give us an idea of how to pilot the spacecraft that would take us to the Moon and back. We spent months rehearsing in these two simulators, so we had a feel for how we would sit, how we would sleep and eat, how we would pilot the spacecraft, and how we would communicate with the many individuals back at Mission Control in Houston.

The Command Module simulator gave us the opportunity to simulate our flight from liftoff to landing. Its console was identical to our real one with switches, displays, dials, controls, and communication equipment. It even had a realistic view out of the window created with a motion picture. In this device we would simulate countdown and launch—and then we'd fly into Earth orbit, go into translunar flight, orbit the Moon, come within feet of a lunar landing, complete a spacecraft rendezvous, and then return home with reentry and splashdown.

In the Lunar Module simulator we could practice a simulation of a lunar landing and imitate flying over the lunar surface, selecting a landing site, and descending and landing on the Moon. We'd then practice flying back to the Command Module.

We also used these simulators to work out all sorts of serious problems we might encounter along the way. This was crucial to learn. Our training instructors would lead us through moment-by-moment scenarios of our Moon missions. At first we'd fly a program straight through without problems. But then, the trainers intentionally tried to challenge us. They would throw in horrific problems for us to solve, like a meteorite hitting our spacecraft or a malfunction in our control systems. It was our responsibility to quickly figure out how to respond to these crises and get used to solving problems in space.

Flying Beds and Mock Moon Rocks

Alan Shepard got a chance to train for our Moon landing in the Lunar Landing Research Vehicle (LLRV), which some people called the "Flying Bedstead," because it looked like an old brass bed frame. This device could actually lift off and fly about 500 feet above the Earth. I never flew this vehicle, but I didn't mind because it was quite dangerous to maneuver.

Many lunar surface simulations were rehearsed at Cape Kennedy in Florida in a specially constructed training area located behind the NASA administrative buildings. We would practice our work wearing pressure suits and backpacks, and we'd rehearse setting up equipment we would later use on the Moon. We often practiced how to pick up Moon rocks by hand or with specially designed handheld equipment. Working in the sweltering heat of the Florida sun was tough, and on some days I would lose up to 10 pounds just from sweating.

The Successes and Failures of Space Travel

Although the Apollo lunar missions were extremely exciting, there were always risks and potential fatalities. We all knew this—my boss, my colleagues, my family, everyone. There were inherent dangers in traveling beyond Earth's orbit and especially in going the distance to the Moon.

My military experience in the Korean War and as a test pilot had prepared me to handle a great deal of dire situations, and I was accustomed to solving difficult problems in flight. I'd been shot at. I'd had equipment break on me. And I knew there were times I was in really tough situations. But if I wanted to be an astronaut, I needed to come to terms with the potential of danger or death. And I did.

Space was a whole new frontier, and there were many unknowns to figure out along the way. We worked hard, had solid contingency plans, and always hoped for the best. But sometimes we failed.

In 1967, only one year after I'd started astronaut training at NASA, tragedy struck. Apollo 1 astronauts Virgil "Gus" Grissom, Edward White, and Roger Chaffee were rehearsing a launch pad test at Kennedy Space Center in Florida on January 27, 1967, in preparation for their upcoming launch date of February 21, 1967.

Suddenly, and without warning, a fire erupted and swept through the Command Module capsule where the astronauts were buckled in their seats. Unable to escape, the three men tragically lost their lives. I was deeply saddened by the loss of my friends and three of Earth's finest space explorers. But I truly believe that Gus, Ed, and Roger would have absolutely wanted us to move forward with the space program.

And in time we did.

Over the next year and a half we worked diligently on correcting potential equipment and spacecraft problems. Apollo missions 7 and 9 were designed to test the Command Module and the Lunar Module spacecraft while orbiting Earth. Apollo missions 8 and 10 orbited the Moon to test equipment and take important lunar photography for the upcoming Apollo missions that would land spacecraft on the Moon.

Contact

On July 20, 1969, Apollo 11 astronaut Neil Armstrong was the first man to set foot on the Moon. Millions of people on Earth tuned in to their radios or turned on their televisions to follow this rare and historic event.

The Apollo 11 crew included Commander Neil Armstrong, Command Module Pilot Michael Collins, and Lunar Module Pilot Buzz Aldrin. The astronauts had a smooth launch from Earth on July 16, 1969, and a few days later, Neil and Buzz were traveling in their Lunar Module named the Eagle and carefully guiding the craft down to their lunar landing site called the Sea of Tranquility.

I remember that summer day in July so well. Charlie Duke was CAPCOM and I was helping out in Mission Control with many of my colleagues. Up to this point the flight had been nearly flawless. But as Neil and Buzz flew the Eagle toward their landing site, they started to have problems.

Neil could see that the Lunar Module was heading toward a dangerous-looking crater, so he took the controls manually to fly the craft away from the crater. This meant that more fuel would be burned, which wasn't good because their fuel was limited and could run out. In addition, alarms starting going off in the craft, which only increased tensions. It seemed like everyone in Mission Control was holding their breath during these last critical seconds.

Fortunately, the alarm problem was determined to be a computer software issue and quickly corrected. And with less than 25 seconds' worth of fuel left, Neil and Buzz landed their craft. "The Eagle has landed!" Neil exclaimed. Everyone in Mission Control breathed a huge sigh of relief. In his iconic southern drawl, Charlie Duke said, "Tranquility, we copy you on the ground. You got a bunch of guys about to turn blue. We're breathing again. Thanks a lot!"

Neil started a video camera attached to the outside of the Lunar Module to film his historic steps. He then slowly stepped down the ladder and onto the Moon. His words will forever be part of history, "That's one small step for man, one giant leap for mankind."

I felt so proud of everyone at NASA and the Apollo program that day. I was especially proud of Neil, Buzz, and Mike. When Apollo 11 splashed down on Earth on July 24, cheers and applause erupted in Mission Control and everyone waved American flags. It was pure and absolute joy. History had been made and we had upheld President Kennedy's challenge to land a man on the Moon and return him safely to Earth before 1971.

About four months later, another Moon mission was good to go. Apollo 12 launched from Kennedy Space Center on November 14, 1969, with a crew that included Commander Charles "Pete" Conrad, Command Module Pilot Richard Gordon, and Lunar Module Pilot Alan Bean. Pete and Alan flew their Lunar Module, the Intrepid, down to the Moon and made a precise landing at the Ocean of Storms. The crew successfully returned to Earth on November 24, 1969.

Apollo 13

> *"Houston, we've had a problem here."* —Astronaut Jack
> Swigert

On April 11, 1970, the Apollo 13 astronauts, James "Jim" Lovell, Jack Swigert, and my good buddy Fred Haise, set out for the Moon. Their lunar landing site was the Fra Mauro Highlands (where the Apollo 14 Lunar Module eventually landed). But about two and a half days after launch when the Apollo 13 crew was nearly 200,000 miles away from Earth, the oxygen tank in their Service Module exploded. This unexpected problem wound up crippling the entire spacecraft by wiping out their vital oxygen and electricity supplies.

Now faced with a terrifying situation, the astronauts needed to figure out a way to breathe, survive, and get back home.

It seemed like everyone on Earth was watching as the dangerous Apollo 13 events unfolded, and people all over the world were anxiously glued to their televisions and radios hoping for the astronauts' safe return.

One of the first things Jim, Jack, and Fred did was to quickly move from the Command Module into the attached Lunar Module. Once they were in this smaller spacecraft, which had some oxygen and electricity, they were then able to shut off and conserve the Command Module's power, oxygen, and fuel that would be crucial to get them back to Earth. In addition, the Lunar Module's engine would also be used to thrust the astronauts around the Moon so they could then get into an orbital path to return home. For all intents and purposes, the Lunar Module became their lifeboat.

Everyone at Mission Control was completely focused on getting the three astronauts back to Earth. And because I knew the Lunar Module inside and out, I was called in to help. I immediately hurried over to a nearby training building that housed the Lunar Module simulator and climbed into the simulator to figure out every maneuver and turn the Apollo 13 astronauts would need to do in their Lunar Module. I had to be one step ahead of them at all times, guiding them as best I could. And if I discovered any problem whatsoever, I would immediately communicate with Mission Control Flight Director Gene Kranz, who would then talk with the astronauts. It was a tense and critical time.

At the same time, astronaut Ken Mattingly was also called in to help. Ken was one of the original three astronauts selected for Apollo 13, and he had trained extensively for this mission. But unfortunately, or fortunately as we later realized, he was grounded due to his exposure to German measles and Jack Swigert had taken his place as Command Module Pilot. Ken climbed into the Command Module simulator that was right next to the Lunar Module simulator and worked through countless procedures, running reentry after reentry under different configurations to help the three astronauts conserve their remaining power and limited oxygen. He focused on how to get them back through the atmosphere of Earth with a marginal oxygen supply. He asked important questions: What could they shut down? What could they turn off? What would they need to do in order to survive?

Jim, Jack, and Fred wound up staying in the Lunar Module, which became very cold, until they got close to Earth. They then climbed back into the Command Module and took their seats. Their next step was to jettison the Lunar Module, which burned up in the atmosphere, before they soared down in the Command Module and plunged into the ocean on April 17, 1970.

It was an extremely difficult time waiting and watching and hoping for the astronauts' return. People all over the world were praying for the three men, and I believe it helped. When I saw the Command Module's bright orange and white striped parachutes open before the capsule plunged into the sea, I felt so relieved. It was finally clear the astronauts had made it home.

Although Apollo 13 never landed on the Moon, the mission was deemed a "successful failure" because the astronauts had returned home safely.

Next on the lineup was my Apollo 14 mission. We were scheduled to head to the Moon just about nine months after Apollo 13 had launched.

Yes, we had a solid crew with Alan Shepard as Commander, Stu Roosa as Command Module Pilot, and I was Lunar Module Pilot. We'd all trained and worked together for years, and we were all experienced and accomplished military men. Alan had earned the rank of rear admiral in the navy, Stu was a colonel in the air force, and I was a captain in the navy. But it was impossible not to think about what might go wrong. I knew that two missions had already made it to the Moon and four men had already walked on the Moon. But would we be able to follow in their footsteps? Or would our spacecraft malfunction like Apollo 13?

6

A Super Long Shot

It was finally time for the Apollo 14 mission to head to the Moon. Our entire trip would last nine days, from January 31 to February 9, 1971. It would take about four days to get to the Moon, two days to work on the lunar surface, and three days to get back home.

All the Apollo Moon missions had backup crews, and ours was made up of astronauts Gene Cernan (Commander), Ron Evans (Command Module Pilot), and Joe Engle (Lunar Module Pilot).

Our Spacecraft

Flying to the Moon was a risky venture, especially since it is a quarter of a million miles away from Earth. To get there, Alan, Stu, and I would ride the massive Saturn V, which was the largest, heaviest, most powerful rocket ever launched on Earth. Standing nearly 363 feet tall (about 60 feet taller than the Statue of Liberty), the rocket weighed about 3,000 tons before liftoff.

Considered one of the most amazing engineering feats of the 20th century, the Saturn V had five engines and used millions of pounds of liquid fuel to thrust our spacecraft into orbit and send it to the Moon. This rocket was launched 13 times from 1967 to 1973 and carried all the Apollo astronauts into space. The final Saturn V launch put Skylab, America's first space station, into orbit in 1973.

Our primary spacecraft, the Kitty Hawk Command Module, was the only part of our entire spacecraft that returned to Earth. This cone-shaped craft was about 13 feet wide and 11 and a half feet tall, and it had five windows and two hatches. Alan, Stu, and I sat in three individual crew stations that were designed as curved couch-like seats, and this is where we piloted the craft, communicated with Mission Control, worked, and ate our meals. We slept in hammocks that were located about one foot beneath our couches. All of our supplies, food, clothing, and the basic equipment we'd need was carefully packed into the walls of the Kitty Hawk.

Another crucial part of our spacecraft was called the Service Module, which was about 13 feet wide and 24 and a half feet long. This cylindrical craft was our basic storehouse for our service and life supporting power systems, and it carried vital supplies such as our oxygen, fuel cells for generating electricity, and necessary fuel tanks. The Service Module was directly connected to the Command Module and referred to as the Command/Service Module, or CSM. Just before splashdown, the Service Module would be jettisoned as the Command Module zoomed to Earth protected by a lifesaving heat shield that could withstand the extremely hot temperatures of reentry.

The Antares Lunar Module was designed with a descent and an ascent stage so that Alan and I could fly down to the Moon and then back up to the Command Module. This meant that the spacecraft needed to have two distinct portions. The upper part of the Antares was where Alan and I would pilot the craft, eat, and sleep while we worked on the Moon. This upper part also housed all of our important life support systems, including guidance and navigation, communications, environmental air control, electrical power, and propulsion.

The lower part of the Antares had four legs with pads for landing, storage bays for equipment, and a ladder so we could climb down to the lunar surface. It held our scientific equipment, a propulsion system, electrical power, water, and oxygen. This lower part would also act as our launch platform so we could lift off and fly back up to the Command Module.

The Bug Barricade and Send-off

Nobody wanted to go way up in space and come down with the flu. So, for three weeks before launch, Alan, Stu, and I were quarantined in biologically sealed crew quarters at the

Kennedy Space Center in Florida. We wanted to avoid catching any germs or bugs from the outside world.

The quarantine area looked like a modest apartment complete with a kitchen, bedrooms, and a living room. We were isolated from most other people and even our families. If we did interact with anyone working on the mission, we'd always have to wear protective biological masks.

But we weren't just sitting around for three weeks watching TV and waiting to fly. Our days were very busy as we rehearsed all of our flight procedures. The three of us would head over to a nearby building and practice launch and in-flight maneuvers in the Command Module simulator. For a great deal of the time, Alan and I practiced different maneuvers in the Lunar Module simulator. These simulators gave us an exciting view of things to come because we could see actual scenes of space and the lunar surface we were about to visit.

When liftoff was just around the corner, it was time to say good-bye to our families. Louise, Karlyn, and Elizabeth flew in from Houston to see me off. But it was a strange and cold farewell without any hugs or kisses. I was still in quarantine, so the four of us had to say good-bye behind a large glass window. Fortunately, there was a sound system so we could communicate.

Family members of the other astronauts were also behind the glass window along with a few dignitaries and celebrities such as Henry Kissinger, who was President Nixon's national security advisor at the time, and actor Kirk Douglas. Elizabeth was overjoyed to see the actor and said, "Oh, Mr. Douglas, I thought you were great in *Spartacus!*" I couldn't help but smile.

T-Minus and Counting!

Launch day arrived, and Alan, Stu, and I were feeling the nervous excitement an athlete might feel before a big football game or a musician might feel before a big performance. We were ready to go and now it was time to play.

That morning we had one last checkup by the medical team before having the traditional astronaut send-off breakfast of steak, eggs, and toast with Deke Slayton, our chief astronaut for the mission, and our backup crew.

Later in the day it was time to suit up. We went to a sanitized area that looked like a laboratory where technicians placed medical devices on our chests that would continually monitor our breathing and heart rate throughout the mission. Next, we put on and zipped up our bulky spacesuits before putting on our helmets and boots. Each one of us also got a handheld oxygen canister so we could breathe with our helmets on.

Now suited up, Alan, Stu, and I rode over to Pad A at Launch Complex 39, in the white NASA minivan. Once we got out of the van I looked over at the enormous rocket towering right in front of us. It was gigantic. I could hear the rocket hissing and rumbling, and it reminded me of an enormous upright steam train waiting at the station, ready to go.

The three of us took the long ride up on the launch pad elevator to our spacecraft sitting at the top of the Saturn V. After stepping out onto a grated catwalk, I looked down at the ground below and could see the beautiful Atlantic Ocean and the pretty white beaches of the Florida coastline. I couldn't believe how high we were. We then headed into an area called the White Room where we reviewed final preparations, put on our escape harnesses, and climbed into the Command Module.

It was great to see astronaut Tom Stafford waiting for us in the White Room. Tom was chief of the Manned Spacecraft Center astronaut office and was there to help with last-minute details. We also met up with our launch pad leader, Guenter Wendt, and his crew, who helped us get into our spacecraft. Guenter liked to wear a bowtie and carry a clipboard, and he was there for all the manned spaceflights. He was also the last person we saw before heading into space.

Climbing into the Kitty Hawk

Guenter had an easygoing nature and made everyone's job easier. As a joke, he handed Alan a cane because Alan was the oldest astronaut to fly to the Moon. This lightheartedness helped relieve some of the natural tension we were all feeling. We took our seats in the Command Module and Guenter's technicians helped buckle us in. We were literally shoulder-to-shoulder now and lying on our backs because the rocket was pointing upward. I sat on the right side of the Command Module, Stu sat in the center seat, and Alan sat on the left side.

We all had specific tasks during the mission. Alan and Stu were responsible for piloting the spacecraft. As systems engineer, my duties included monitoring our power supply and air pressure, and overseeing all the instruments on the right side of the cockpit that measured the spacecraft's functions.

"Godspeed to you all!" Guenter said, smiling broadly. Then, without another word, he shut our hatch with a loud thud and locked it. At last it was just the three of us. We didn't just take off; we had about two hours before launch. Alan, Stu, and I anxiously awaited countdown.

Unfortunately, countdown was delayed. An afternoon thunderstorm was brewing, so Mission Control wanted us to hold off and let the storm pass. Of course it was hard to wait because we were so pumped up to fly. But we knew NASA was being cautious. Lightning could be big trouble. I immediately remembered the problem the Apollo 12 team had during launch. Lightning had hit their rocket during liftoff and shut down some of their most important systems. Fortunately, as their rocket surged into space, the astronauts were able to correct the problem and their mission turned out to be a big success.

But sitting in our cramped, dark, and cold Command Module with a weather delay was rough. I chatted with Alan and Stu and tried to stay positive, not knowing how long the storm would last. I focused on rehearsing our launch sequence. But then I started to think about Louise and the girls sitting in the bleachers anxiously waiting for liftoff. I wondered how they were doing and if they were getting soaked by any rain. I thought about my mom and dad, Sandra and Jay, my grandparents, little Oscar, and the thousands of people watching our launch.

And then I just dozed off for a little while.

After 40 minutes the skies cleared, and we were finally cleared to go. Hearing countdown was incredible. I could feel the tremendous rush of excitement. "15, 14, 13, 12, 11, 10, 9, 8 . . . initial sequence start . . . 5, 4, 3, 2, 1, 0. Launch commit. LIFTOFF!"

And suddenly we had liftoff at exactly 4:03 PM on that amazing Sunday afternoon.

As our rocket ignited, gigantic orange clouds and white-hot fiery flames blasted from the five engines, sending us straight up amidst a powerful and deafening roar.

"Beautiful," Alan said.

"Go, baby, go!" Stu called out.

"She's going, she's going," I added. "Everything's good."

It took a lot of force to lift our extremely heavy rocket up from the launch pad and out into orbit. Inside our Command Module, however, it seemed eerily quiet. With our helmets on we could only hear communication from Mission Control and each other. As we lifted I felt some pressure push against my chest and back, but I focused on everything I was supposed to do and did it. Once again I remembered Grandpa Bull's reassuring words, *Steady as she goes, Edgar. Steady as she goes.*

Capsule Communicator

During our entire mission, Alan, Stu, and I were in constant communication with the Capsule Communicator, more commonly known as the CAPCOM, who was stationed at Mission Control Center in Houston during flight and reentry. Typically, the CAPCOM was one of the support crew astronauts or one of the backup crew astronauts. Because our mission lasted nine days, we had a number of different CAPCOMS including Fred Haise (we liked to call him "Freddo"), who was the Lunar Module (LM) Checkout and Separation CAPCOM; Bruce McCandless, the Lunar Landing and Extravehicular Activity-1 CAPCOM; and Gordon Fullerton (nicknamed

"Gordo"), who served as the Planning Shift CAPCOM. Deke Slayton would sometimes take over as CAPCOM, as would our backup crew astronauts.

In addition, I was a CAPCOM for the Apollo 15 Moon mission in 1971 and the Apollo 16 Moon mission in 1972.

Three Critical Stages of Liftoff

Our Saturn V rocket was built with an ingenious three-part system that would take us higher and move us faster than any rocket in history. Once we lifted to a certain altitude, the lowest part of our rocket would separate and drop into the ocean. And as we continued to lift up and away from Earth, another large part of our rocket would separate and also drop into the ocean. Finally, we'd let go of a third and final portion that would be jettisoned into space.

Everything on our spacecraft was computerized, including the three stages of liftoff, our entire flight plan, our Moonwalk, and return to Earth. Many, many computer programmers had helped make our extraordinary mission a reality.

During liftoff, I looked over at Alan and noticed his hand was on the abort button. He was prepared to abort the mission if anything went wrong at this critical moment. Liftoff was extremely dangerous because we were sitting on top of tons of highly explosive fuel. So in the event of an emergency, the abort button would set into motion an escape procedure that would hoist the Command Module off the rocket stack so we could parachute back to Earth. Fortunately, this didn't happen.

For the next two and a half minutes we traveled very high above Earth at about 6,000 miles per hour. As I glanced out my window I could see the eastern coastlines of North Carolina and South Carolina, and the Caribbean. And it wasn't long before I could see the actual curve of the planet. It was absolutely beautiful to look down at the soft white clouds and the sparkling blue waters below.

But there wasn't a lot of time for sightseeing. We needed to focus on flying. The second stage of liftoff used two engines and lasted about six minutes. We more than doubled our speed to 16,000 miles per hour as we sailed about 115 miles above Earth. I wasn't looking out the window at this point; my focus was strictly on monitoring the gauges on my instrument panel. The third stage used only one engine and lasted about two and a half minutes. Now we were being hurtled through space at 17,500 miles per hour.

But before heading out into deep space, we orbited the Earth one and a half times in a special safety measure called "Go, no go." This gave us about two and a half hours to make sure everything was working right.

"Will you look at that?" I said to Stu and Alan as I looked out the window at the world below. From this unique vantage point, high above Earth, I could see entire continents and oceans from above. It was absolutely remarkable to see. "Isn't it something?" Stu replied.

Trans-lunar Injection—A Powerful Boost

After about two and a half hours into the flight we heard our CAPCOM say, "You're GO for the Moon. GO for TLI," and we knew we were good to go. But we needed a lot more power to propel us out of Earth's gravitational pull. So when we were flying over Australia, we ignited our engine again for a procedure called Trans-lunar Injection that sent us rocketing to the super speed of about 24,500 miles per hour. It was a powerful surge that threw us back against our crew stations. But it also gave us the enormous thrust that pushed us on our path toward to the Moon and to the point where the Moon's gravitational pull would begin to dominate. Everything was going exactly as planned, and Alan, Stu, and I were feeling good about that. At least for a little while. Our next big step nearly ended our entire flight.

A Terrible Time

We'd been flying for about three hours and now it was time to retrieve and link up with the Lunar Module spacecraft that had been carefully brought along in the rocket stack.

In a procedure called Transposition and Docking, we needed to attach the nose of the Lunar Module to the nose of the Command Module. This was Stu's job. Stu had practiced Transposition and Docking over and over again on Earth in the Command Module simulator and had truly mastered the simulation. But now it was time to do it for real, way out in the vast sea of space.

Using thrusters like miniature engines, Stu piloted the Command Module away from the rocket stack. Large panels of the rocket then opened up like a flower, exposing the top of the Lunar Module. Stu backed the Command Module away and slowly rotated us about 180 degrees so we were lined up with the Lunar Module. Now it was time for Stu to move the two crafts together with careful precision.

Unfortunately, things didn't go as planned and the next hour or so was agonizing. Stu had positioned the two spacecraft just right, but for whatever reason, the capture latches would not lock the Lunar Module with the Command Module.

Stu kept trying and trying—one time, two times, three times, four times, and even a fifth time with absolutely no luck. His heart rate was starting to soar and it was easy to see he was getting stressed. "We're unable to get a capture," I told Mission Control, hardly able to believe we were having so much trouble.

Al and I tried to reassure Stu, but everyone knew that if we couldn't dock the two spacecraft, our mission was over. I just couldn't believe we'd been faced with such a big problem after only a few hours. We needed to come up with a solution. And fast.

Stu, Alan and I took a break from the Transposition and Docking procedure, and started to work on a solution with Mission Control. Nobody was sure what was wrong, but we wondered if the pre-launch thunderstorm had caused ice to build up within the spacecraft docking latches and caused the problem. Finally, Mission Control encouraged Stu to try again in a slightly different way. This time he was to use extra force with the thrusters while Alan flipped a switch to retract the docking mechanism. Stu and Alan both tried the new idea and it worked. Finally, we could hear the sweet sounds of the docking latches snapping shut.

"We had a hard dock, Houston." Alan exclaimed. Everybody was relieved and there was a lot of clapping back at Mission Control. I was so glad we hadn't given up. A little ingenuity can go a long way, especially when you're a long way from home.

And I sure hoped this would be our last close call.

Smooth Sailing Ahead?

At last, after about five hours, we were well on our way to the Moon. Our Saturn V rocket had blasted us into space and had gone through its critical three stages. We'd had success with Trans-lunar Injection and eventually with Transposition and Docking. And now the Lunar Module was stationed at the very tip of our Command Module, just where it was supposed to be.

As we moved farther and farther away, we could see our whole planet in its magnificence. It was a powerful sight. Earth looked like a brilliant blue and white sphere suspended in the inky blackness of space. Some people have described it as a "big, blue marble."

I could see the thin, white ring of Earth's atmosphere, and it reminded me of the rind of a piece of fruit. Although I knew it contained all our oxygen and everything we need to live, Earth's atmosphere just looked so thin and fragile. And as we traveled away, we saw Earth getting smaller and smaller as the Moon appeared larger and larger. I thought about Buck Rogers and all his daring space adventures. Only this time, I was the adventurer.

At this point in the mission we could finally take off our bulky spacesuits, helmets, and boots and pack them away in bags for the time being. We always wore our spacesuits during critical parts of the mission such as liftoff, flying in the Lunar Module, and walking on the Moon. But right now, we loved being able to put on our lighter, full-body coveralls, which were a heck of a lot more comfortable.

Although we were flying fast, it almost felt like we were standing still inside the spacecraft. Being in a weightless

environment was such an unusual experience. Everything
needed to be buckled or bolted down, or it would simply float
around the cabin. Astronauts included. The first time I took
out my pen and let it go, it was fascinating to watch it float by
my eyes. Concepts like up and down didn't seem to exist, and
it was a strange sensation to unbuckle myself from my couch
and float around in the cabin. Just the slightest push from the
instrument panel or my seat would send me floating away.
Some of the astronauts had motion sickness in zero G, but I
realized that if I kept my mind occupied I didn't feel queasy.

Now moving ahead on our invisible path to the Moon,
our spacecraft didn't move forward like an airplane. Instead,
it slowly rotated around and around in what we called the
"barbeque mode." This way, the side of the spacecraft that
was facing the sun wouldn't get too hot, and the side that
wasn't facing the sun wouldn't get too cold. The slow rota-
tion method, technically called passive thermal control, was
the only way we could travel to the Moon and maintain our
spacecraft's thermal balance.

The three of us settled into our individual eating, sleeping,
and work routines that were carefully programmed ahead of
time. We were always busy running the ship and studying
our checklists and plans. Sometimes we took sightings from
the stars to keep the navigation platform aligned, and we
were always in constant communication with Mission Control. During downtime we'd inspect our equipment, peer out
through our telescope at the stars, and sometimes we'd relax
and listen to music. I brought along songs from the Broadway
hit *My Fair Lady*, which I really liked.

Space Food

Traveling to the Moon took a lot of energy—the energy to launch our rocket, the energy to keep our spacecraft running, and the energy to nourish us. But finding foods we could eat in space wasn't easy. Initially there was some worry we might choke while trying to swallow food in zero G. Scientists also wondered if the human body could digest food in a weightless environment. But our bodies functioned just as they did on Earth. Since we didn't have a kitchen onboard and there was limited space on the craft, our foods needed to be compact, easy to prepare, and nutritious. And because we were dining in zero G, our food couldn't float away before it ever reached our mouths.

The NASA chefs and food scientists came up with clever ways to prepare and serve all our meals, snacks, and beverages so we were able to eat. Before liftoff, Alan, Stu, and I were given a list of about 70 different foods and beverages and asked to choose menus for our nine-day voyage. We sampled a lot of space food ahead of time. There were some tasty sounding choices like lobster bisque and peach ambrosia. But there was no getting around the fact that what we ate was freeze-dried food in plastic see-through pouches that came equipped with a straw or spoon. Long story short—it definitely wasn't Mama's cooking. At least we weren't chowing down on freeze-dried frogs, lizards, or bugs we'd learned about during our desert and rain forest training.

The process of freeze-drying removed water from our foods. It helped make everything small and easy to store, prepare, and eat. We'd simply pop open a bag and add hot or cold water. After about 10 to 15 minutes, some version of soup, pasta, or fruit drink would appear. We got our hot and cold water from a nifty squirt gun-like device located next to our couches, and we'd squirt water either directly into our mouths or into our food packets. We also used a "spoon bowl," where food came in zip-lock bags. This food was sticky enough that it wouldn't float off the spoon.

I liked the cinnamon toast that came shaped like a small cube and the vacuum-packed roast beef sandwiches. I wasn't crazy about some of the mushy stuff like beef stew in a baggie. Overall the food was fine, and I didn't lose any weight during the entire mission.

Way to Go

The one question I am asked over and over again as an Apollo astronaut is "How do you go to the bathroom in space?" I always answer "very carefully," and this gets a big laugh. But the fact is, nature calls, even on the way to the Moon.

Getting rid of human waste in weightlessness was another aspect of space travel that definitely had to be solved. If we couldn't capture our urine, for example, we'd have yellow globules floating around the capsule, and that would be awful. So, we used a condom-like device to collect our urine. We'd transfer it from a urine transfer tube and into a tank, before it was released out into space. Curiously enough, the urine froze and had an iridescent sparkle when it was vented out into space.

Solid waste was a different matter and there were a number of steps we needed to follow. First, we emptied our waste

CAFÉ ZERO G

Enjoying breakfast, lunch, and dinner in space required a great deal of creativity during the Apollo Moon missions. It's not easy moving food from a variety of containers into one's mouth in zero gravity. And because it was a tight fit in the Command Module and the Lunar Module, meals were freeze-dried and vacuum-packed to save space.
Here was a typical Apollo 14 menu for four days in space.

	Meal A—Breakfast	Meal B—Lunch	Meal C—Dinner
DAY 1	Peaches Bacon Squares Strawberry Cubes Orange Drink	Beef & Potatoes Butterscotch Pudding Brownies Grape Punch	Salmon Salad Chicken & Rice Sugar Cookie Cubes Cocoa Pineapple-Grapefruit Drink
DAY 2	Fruit Cocktail Sausage Patties Cinnamon Toast Cubes Cocoa Grapefruit Drink	Frankfurters Applesauce Chocolate Pudding Orange-Grapefruit Drink	Spaghetti & Meat Sauce Pork & Scalloped Potatoes Pineapple Fruit Cake Grape Punch
DAY 3	Peaches Bacon Squares Apricot Cereal Cubes Grape Drink Orange Drink	Cream of Chicken Soup Turkey & Gravy Cheese Cracker Cubes Chocolate Cubes Pineapple-Grapefruit Drink	Tuna Salad Chicken Stew Butterscotch Pudding Cocoa Grapefruit Drink
DAY 4	Canadian Bacon Sugar Coated Corn Flakes Peanut Cubes Cocoa Orange-Grapefruit Drink	Shrimp Cocktail Ham & Potatoes Fruit Cocktail Date Fruit Cake Grapefruit Drink	Beef Stew Coconut Cubes Banana Pudding Grape Punch

into special plastic fecal bags. Then we added a capsule of blue germicide and mixed all the contents together before placing the waste in another bag. Each bag was then stored onboard in a sanitation box for later disposal on Earth.

If all of this sounds unpleasant, it was. But it was a necessary procedure and it worked.

Another hygienic challenge was bathing, or the lack of it. We couldn't take a bath or shower during the entire nine days. But we did have wet wipes to clean our skin, and disposable toothbrushes with edible toothpaste. We'd brush our teeth, swallow the toothpaste, and then throw away the brushes.

Sleep Time and ESP

Sleep was also a tricky situation on the craft, and we always made sure one person was awake and on watch. While two of us slept, the other astronaut piloted the craft and communicated with Mission Control. To catch some shut-eye, I'd pull myself below my couch and climb into my sleeping bag. Because we were in zero G, we didn't need a pillow or a mattress to rest our head or body. We'd simply float into dreamland. And fortunately, small window shades helped shut out the sunlight and give us a sense of nighttime.

The Apollo astronauts were allowed to bring along reading material and music to enjoy during downtime or before our sleep periods. So I decided to get creative. One night when I was supposed to be sleeping while Stu was on watch, Stu called out for me. "Hey there, Ed," he said. "What's going on?" It was about 45 minutes past lights out, but he could see my flashlight was on.

EXTRASENSORY PERCEPTION

Can we know what someone else is thinking without saying a word? Those who believe in extrasensory perception, or ESP, say it's possible. The concept, sometimes referred to as the "sixth sense," became popular through the work of Dr. Joseph Banks Rhine, a psychologist from Duke University. Dr. Rhine founded the Duke University Parapsychology Lab in 1930 to study ESP, which comprises three different kinds of phenomena: telepathy (communication of thoughts from one person to another without the use of the five senses), clairvoyance (recognizing objects or events without the use of the five senses), and precognition (being able to know the future). Since Dr. Rhine's studies, a great deal of research has been conducted to better understand extrasensory perception. Today, some scientists believe ESP is based on properties of quantum physics where information can be exchanged on subatomic levels.

"Not much," I replied.

Actually, I was conducting a long-distance ESP experiment that only a few other people in the world knew about. Not even Alan or Stu knew about it.

In addition to being a space explorer, I also wanted to explore consciousness and the mind. I was very curious about ESP, which is the ability to know or perceive something beyond the five senses. Some people refer to this as having a hunch, or having intuition. For example, if the phone rings and you think you know who is calling, this may be an example of ESP. I was especially curious about the research of scientist Dr. Joseph Banks Rhine, whose work focused on paranormal subjects. Dr. Rhine's research suggested that ESP can work close-up, but I wondered whether this phenomenon could happen hundreds of thousands of miles away. In space!

I realized that flying to the Moon gave me a chance to test this hypothesis. So, on four different nights (two nights on the way to the Moon and two nights returning from the Moon) I took out a pen and pad of paper connected to a small knee-board near my sleeping bag. I would write down a sequence of numbers and matching symbols at a specific time. I would then carefully concentrate on what I'd written for exactly seven minutes, almost as if I were memorizing my notes.

Back on Earth, at exactly the same time, two doctors and two psychics were also writing down their own sequence of numbers and matching symbols and concentrating on what they'd written for exactly seven minutes. When I returned from the Moon, we'd all compare notes and see if ESP had worked from thousands of miles away. I couldn't wait to find out.

After I was done with my evening science project, I turned off my flashlight.

"Goodnight," Stu said. He'd obviously noticed my light was out.

"Night," I replied. I then closed my eyes and started to focus on the big adventure that was just around the corner.

(left) I was born in 1930 in Hereford, Texas. Here I am in Hereford at the home of my Grandmother Mitchell when I was about three years old.
Courtesy Edgar Mitchell

(below) In 1935 my family moved to Roswell, New Mexico, where my father was a rancher. I'm riding my Shetland pony, Sparky.
Courtesy Edgar Mitchell

The Apollo 14 Crew: Command Module Pilot Stu Roosa (left), Commander Alan Shepard (center), and Lunar Module Pilot Edgar Mitchell (right). *Courtesy NASA*

Roswell Daily Record

Movies as Usual

Claims Army Is Slacking Courts Martial

RAAF Captures Flying Saucer On Ranch in Roswell Region

Indiana Senator Lays Protest Before Patterson

House Passes Tax Slash by Large Margin

Security Council Paves Way to Talks On Arms Reductions

No Details of Flying Disk Are Revealed

Ex-King Carol Weds Mme. Lupescu

Some of Soviet Satellites May Attend Paris Meeting

Roswell Hardware Man and Wife Report Disk Seen

(above) In 1947, when I was 17, I was shocked to learn that an alleged flying saucer had landed on a ranch not too far from my home. The next day the *Roswell Daily Record* reported the saucer was a weather balloon. Later in life I realized this incident piqued my curiosity about ETs and space.
Courtesy Roswell Daily Record

(right) I've loved airplanes and flying since I was young. After college I enlisted in the navy and began flight training in Pensacola, Florida. I'm standing on the wing of an AT-6 SNJ "Texan" navy trainer.
Courtesy Edgar Mitchell

(left) Apollo astronauts needed to know how to survive in harsh environments in the event we crash-landed or were stranded. We learned to survive in the Panama jungles. Here I'm busy chopping down a palm tree to access the heart of the palm, which was the edible core.
Courtesy NASA

(above) In sweltering Florida heat, Alan and I practiced the work we would do on the Moon in our spacesuits. On some days I could lose up to ten pounds simply by sweating.
Courtesy NASA

(left) Standing 363 feet tall, our massive and mighty Saturn V rocket thrust us on our way to the Moon.
Courtesy NASA

(right) Our Moon journey was made possible via the combined spacecraft of the cone-shaped Command Module powered by the cylindrical Service Module.
Courtesy NASA

Space food was freeze-dried and vacuum-packed to make it as compact as possible. Here is a cheese sandwich used for the Apollo Moon missions. *Courtesy NASA*

Our cone-shaped Kitty Hawk Command Module was our primary spacecraft while flying to the Moon and back to Earth. It was a tight fit for three grown men. *Courtesy Kennedy Space Center Visitor Complex*

This Apollo 16 photo shows something humans never see while on Earth—the desolate far side of the Moon. Alan and I orbited to the far side of the Moon when our abort signal malfunctioned. *Courtesy NASA*

The Apollo 14 Antares Lunar Module, our home away from home, where Alan and I slept, ate, and worked while on the Moon. *Courtesy NASA*

Seeing Earth from the Moon was a beautiful sight to behold and a life-changing event for me. This fantastic photo of earthrise was taken in July 1969 during the Apollo 8 Mission. *Courtesy NASA*

(above) Once Alan and I set foot on the lunar surface on February 5, 1971, we took one another's photo while standing by the American flag.
Courtesy NASA

(right) On the Moon there is one-sixth the gravitational pull of Earth. As I hike to Cone Crater, I carefully study my checklist, which is a minute-by-minute account of my Moon work.
Courtesy NASA

Immediately after our Command Module hit the choppy South Pacific waters on February 9, 1971, navy frogmen were right there to retrieve us. Alan, Stu, and I sit in the orange life raft and wear protective masks. *Courtesy NASA*

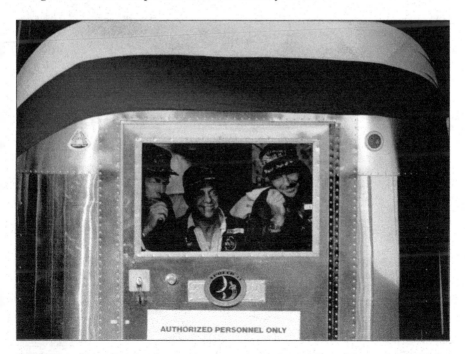

AUTHORIZED PERSONNEL ONLY

After returning to Earth, Alan, Stu, and I peer out the window of the Mobile Quarantine Facility. *Courtesy NASA*

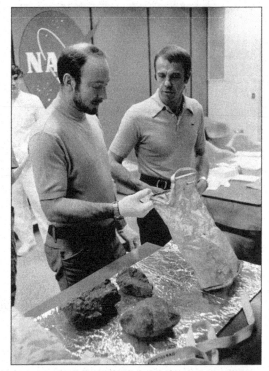

(right) In the Lunar Receiving Laboratory (LRL) at the Manned Spacecraft Center in Houston, Texas, Alan and I study and catalog some of the many Moon rocks we brought back home.
Courtesy NASA

(below) This family photo was taken a few weeks before the Apollo 14 Moon mission. Louise Mitchell (left) with Elizabeth Mitchell, Karlyn Mitchell, me, and our terrier, Whiskers.
Courtesy NASA

The Rocky Road Down

> *"Sometimes your only available transportation is a leap of faith."*
>
> —*Margaret Shepard*

It was day four and we'd been traveling for about 80 hours. I had a scruffy beard, I needed a bath, and a slice of non freeze-dried hot apple pie was sounding mighty good. But my thoughts were focused elsewhere. I could barely keep my eyes off the incredibly enormous object just outside our window that we were hurtling toward.

"The old Moon is sure getting big in the commander's window," I said to Mission Control.

"Roger, Ed."

The flight controllers and engineers at Mission Control always enjoyed hearing from us. But they were busy with the newest part of our journey, which meant helping us slow down the Kitty Hawk and move into lunar orbit. It was an exciting time as we neared our destination.

Once we were in orbit around the Moon, there was so much to see. It was great to look out the window and be able to spot some of the craters, such as Cone Crater and Doublet, we'd learned about in our training. The major craters all had names, and as lunar explorers we wanted to share what we saw with everyone at Houston.

"Well, this really is a wild place, up here," Alan said. "It has all the grays, browns, whites, and dark craters that everybody's talked about before. It's really quite a sight. No atmosphere at all."

Alan was right. The lack of atmosphere on the Moon made the layout of the land crystal clear and easy to see. The Moon had a distinct, unusual look. The Earth is colorfully blue and white and seems to glisten in space, while the Moon looks like its polar opposite. I told Mission Control I thought it seemed as if the Moon had been molded out of grayish plaster of paris and then dusted with colors of browns and more grays.

The far side of the Moon has its own unique look with long, dark shadows and a stark, desolate appearance. Later that day as we continued to orbit, I saw my first earthrise. *Earthrise*, I thought. *I'm not looking at a sunrise; I'm looking at an earthrise.*

"It's a beautiful sight to see Earth from here," I told Mission Control.

Finally it was time for Alan and me to put on our spacesuits again and move out of the Command Module and into the Lunar Module. Alan and I grabbed our spacesuits out of the bags where we'd stowed them, and about 30 minutes later we were suited up and ready to go. The two of us pulled ourselves down into the tunnel that led from the Command Module into the Lunar Module. We opened the hatch and went inside our new lunar home. Once we'd looked over the craft to make sure everything was in order, we took our places in front of the instrument panel. I stood on the right side and Alan stood on the left.

It was a tight fit and our cabin was small because the Antares needed to be as compact and lightweight as possible. In zero gravity, there really isn't sitting or standing, there is only floating. So we saved space and weight by standing up the entire time without the use of large seats. As we stood, special straps were used to anchor our feet.

Stu was waiting at the hatch, ready to shut and lock it. Normally Stu was cheerful and easygoing, but at this moment he looked concerned and I imagined he was thinking, *Will I ever see these two guys again?*

It wasn't easy to break up our three-man team, but this was the only way any of the Apollo astronauts could complete their missions. Two guys would fly down to the Moon while one guy remained in the spacecraft, orbiting above the Moon and waiting for the two others to return.

Stu wished us well, and then closed and locked the hatch. After all my work in the design and testing of the Lunar Module at Grumman Aircraft in Long Island, and after practicing over and over again in the Lunar Module simulator, it was now time to see if this unique flying machine would work. I sure hoped it would.

The first thing we needed to do was undock the Lunar Module from the Command Module in a procedure called Command/Service Module–Lunar Module, or "CSM-LM" Separation. To do this, Stu first flew us down into a lower orbit that was about 10 miles above the surface of the Moon.

Once we'd moved down to the lower orbit, Alan and I had to carefully back the Lunar Module away from the Command Module with Stu's help.

"Okay, okay—you're moving out and you're hanging on the end of the probe," Stu said. "Okay, we seem real steady. I'm going to back off from you."

Then Stu added, "And, we're free."

Thank heavens this all went very smoothly. Once the Antares was a completely separate spacecraft, Stu then flew the Kitty Hawk back up to a higher orbit, which was about 60 miles above the Moon. At this higher orbit, Stu continued to orbit the Moon and was busy taking pictures and mapping the lunar surface for future Apollo missions.

Alan and I were now on our own in the Antares. We wore our spacesuits the entire time, but we took off our helmets, gloves, and boots to feel more comfortable during our rest periods.

Abort! Abort?

Before heading down to the lunar surface, Alan and I were directed to fly the Lunar Module around the Moon two times to make sure everything was working exactly as it should. It took about two hours to travel one orbit around the Moon, so our two orbits would equal about four hours. If we had a problem at this critical stage, we could use our abort procedure, which would automatically shoot us back up to Stu in the Command Module. Of course, this was the last thing we wanted to do. We wanted to walk on the Moon.

As we orbited, we could look down at the lunar surface, and we had excellent and highly accurate maps that showed us exactly where our Fra Mauro landing site was. From Earth, Fra Mauro is located just west of the center of the Moon.

But landing on the Moon was a complex feat. We had very specific procedures to follow that would land us exactly where we needed to go. A lot was at stake and we had to get it right. There was noticeable tension in our Lunar Module, and I'm sure it was the same at Mission Control.

When we were halfway through one lunar orbit, Alan and I were flying on the far side, or the backside, of the Moon. Here we had a complete communication blackout with Mission Control because there was no way to get a radio signal. Not being able to talk with Mission Control made the journey risky, and we all knew this. But there was no way around it.

As we continued to orbit the Moon, we flew our craft right over our landing site. Alan and I were so happy to see it. Everything seemed fine and we felt like we were right on track. But then, as I talked about in the introduction, something went terribly wrong.

Suddenly and without warning, a mysterious abort signal from our computer guidance system cropped up on our instrument panel. Alan and I immediately let Mission Control know about it, but because MC always knew everything that happened at every moment during our flight, they were already aware of the problem.

Imagine being so far from Earth and so close to the Moon and seeing a bright red abort light go on. Was it a false alarm or was it the real deal? The abort mode was necessary because it provided a safety net if something went wrong and we needed to make a fast getaway. But right now, the last thing we wanted to see was an ominous-looking abort light.

At first NASA engineers wondered if the abort signal had been triggered because a floating solder ball had lodged in the abort switch. Fred Haise, our CAPCOM during this time, immediately radioed me. "Ed, tap on the instrument panel with your pen light."

"Okay, Freddo," I replied and tapped away. And just like that the abort light went off.

"Good work, Ed," Fred told me. And we all felt relieved.

But then the abort light came right back on.

No need to panic, I told myself. Alan and I waited for Mission Control to tell us what to do next. We were eventually instructed to continue flying around the Moon while Houston worked on a solution. So Alan and I continued on our orbital path.

When we were flying on the far side, I peered down at the eerie-looking craters with their intense black and white shadows and wondered what I'd gotten myself into. It was bad enough when we had so much trouble with Transposition and Docking. But now this. I knew Louise would know what was going on and I hoped she wasn't worried. We'd solved problems before on our flight and I knew we'd solve this one too. I had faith. Plus, I knew the Lunar Module like the back of my hand, and this gave me confidence.

It was two in the morning in Houston and somebody had to come up with an idea right away.

Fortunately, the engineers at Mission Control phoned Don Eyles, the young, longhaired computer whiz from MIT in Massachusetts who had written all the guidance control software for the Lunar Module including the abort code. Don knew the program thoroughly, and just as the folks in Houston suspected, he was wide awake and paying close attention to the Apollo 14 mission.

After discussing the problem with MC, Don came up with the idea of reprogramming the Lunar Module's onboard computer so it would be instructed to ignore the abort signal. Don got right to work; he had less than two hours to write out a whole new code and get us out of this terrible jam. To make sure his idea was sound, Don wisely tested the code in the Lunar Module simulator at the MIT lab. It worked.

Don gave the new code sequence to Mission Control in Houston, who then relayed the new code to me. As I listened to the numbers being called out to me, I ever so carefully keyed them into our computer. I didn't have time to panic, lose control, or mess up. I had to get it right and there couldn't be a single mistake. I calmed down by telling myself, *This is just like a simulation. You can do this.*

Once the new code was punched in, it worked exactly as we hoped it would. The abort signal light went off. But there was a big hitch. We realized that if we ever did need to escape, we no longer had an automatic abort system and we'd have to perform the abort sequence manually.

Another Close Call

The abort signal malfunction had slowed us down and time was running out. Our task was now to carefully begin the descent to the lunar surface at Fra Mauro. Everything was working. We were almost there.

But then something new went wrong.

Our landing radar, which indicated how close or far we were from the lunar surface, did not go on when it was supposed to. And we simply could not land the Antares without the landing radar. I could feel my adrenaline pumping, but I was the Lunar Module Pilot and it was my responsibility to handle this new ordeal. Alan looked over at me and we just shook our heads in disbelief. I knew Alan was a solid crewmate and was glad to be with him at this critical moment.

Alan had already made history as the very first American in space aboard the Mercury program Freedom 7 flight. But after that historic flight, Alan faced big setbacks that got in the way of his dreams. An inner ear disease had grounded him from flying for years until he had delicate inner ear surgery that corrected the problem. Once Alan was okay again, he was selected to be commander for Apollo 14. Like me, Alan truly wanted to walk on the Moon and he'd worked hard to get to this point. We were so close and we didn't want something like failed landing radar to get in our way.

Mission Control was on it. Fred radioed and informed us that rewriting the abort signal computer code had, unfortunately, interfered with the landing radar. But without this radar we had no way to accurately determine our altitude above the surface. Our Fra Mauro landing site was a rugged area filled with craters, small hills, and valleys. Plus, Mission Control rules would not allow a landing without the radar. That's just the way it was.

"Come on, radar!" I said as if it could hear. "Lock on!"

Mission Control came up with yet another solution: Fred told Alan to cycle the circuit breaker that provided power for the landing radar. Alan cycled the switch immediately.

"Come on!" I said again, almost commanding the radar to work.

And just like that, in the nick of time, the radar started up and locked in. We looked at our computers and could see we were headed exactly where we were supposed to be. We hadn't gotten off course at all.

Alan and I were in an unusual position while heading down to the Moon. Up until this point we had been flying on our backs as we stood in the Antares. We could literally see the sky and stars out our window. But at about 10,000 feet above the lunar surface, we started to pitch over, which meant our spacecraft was turning and moving into an upright position to land.

Happy with the pitch over, Alan exclaimed, "We're right on the money."

I could immediately see Cone Crater and it was an incredible sight.

Seconds later, we got the green light from Mission Control. "Houston, you're go for landing."

"Here we go," Alan said. "Shoot for the Moon, Ed."

"Looks real good," I added. At 3,000 feet above the lunar surface, I started to give continual updates of our descent. "2,048 feet, coming down a little fast," I said. "2,050 feet a second, little bit fast, but not bad. "1,500. Little fast, not bad. Over."

"Starting down, starting down," Alan said. "We're in good shape, too."

"Going down, looking great."

"Sixty seconds."

"Three feet per second—40 feet," I said. "Three feet per second—30. Three feet per second, looking great. Twenty feet. Ten. Three feet per second . . . Contact, Al." And there was a bump as the footpads of the Antares hit the Moon.

"Stop. Auto. Auto!" Alan called out.

"We're on the surface," I said. It was February 5, 1971, at 4:18 AM, Eastern Standard Time. We were on the Moon.

"Okay, we've made a good landing," Alan said.

"Roger, Antares," Fred replied.

I felt elated we'd made it right on our landing site. "That was a beautiful one," I added. And indeed it was. We had landed in a little crater and the Antares was tilted on a bit of a slope, but we'd done it. I had an enormous feeling of relief and complete happiness, and I imagine the cheering, hooting, and hollering down at Mission Control might have been heard around the world. I could just see Louise and the girls jumping for joy. I knew my family was proud of me, and I bet that Don Eyles, Guenter and his team, everyone at NASA, and everyone back home were thrilled.

There was no mistaking the fact that Alan and I had landed. We were the third manned mission to make it to the Moon, and it felt tremendous.

8

A Marvelous Day for a Moonwalk

"Toto, I've a feeling we're not in Kansas anymore."
—Dorothy, The Wizard of Oz

Even though we were 240,000 miles from home, it was great to be on solid ground again. And we had arrived on the Moon at just the right time. Because lunar temperatures could be extremely hot or cold, it made sense to land our spacecraft when the Sun was low in the sky for two big reasons. The early morning Sun created long shadows on the lunar surface, which made it easier to see during our landing. It also wouldn't be so incredibly hot while we were working on the Moon.

Although Alan and I had a challenging ride down to Fra Mauro, I couldn't wait to get out of the Antares and walk around. I immediately started to peer out the window at this new world. My first thought was that the Moon looked like a desolate and inhospitable desert, like some of the most barren regions of New Mexico where I grew up. Of course there wasn't a creature, plant, blade of grass, flower, or tree in sight. I could see the lunar surface had a soft, rolling terrain with many large and small craters and rocks scattered about. Everything was covered with a grayish, powdery Moon dust, and there was a stark but magnificent beauty about it.

It wasn't long before Alan and I heard from CAPCOM Bruce McCandless, who asked us to describe our new surroundings with as much detail as possible. I thought about all my geology training and remembered my instructor telling us to be the "eyes and ears" for everyone back home. I was eager to take a stab at describing the lunar surface and gave it my best shot.

A great deal of what the astronauts said during their unique Moon missions was recorded for historical purposes and archived as NASA mission transcripts. The following excerpts are from the "Apollo 14 Technical Air-to-Ground Voice Transmission" document and are the conversations that took place among Bruce McCandless in Houston, and Alan Shepard and I as we looked out our Lunar Module window and described the unusual new setting before us. As Alan and I talked about what we viewed, we used clock time to describe the locations of the primary craters, Doublet, Cone, and Triplet, we were about to explore.

And because one of our LM footpads had landed in a crater and tilted our spacecraft, Bruce asked Alan about this first.

04-13-45-24 (Bruce McCandless) CAPCOM
Antares, this is Houston. We're standing by for your description of the lunar surface as viewed from the windows of the Lunar Module, and we'd also be interested

specifically in hearing whether you feel that the roll in the spacecraft is due primarily to terrain or whether you feel that there is some landing gear stroking, also. Over.

04-13-45-50 (Alan Shepard: Commander)

Okay. We'll be right with you on the condition of the lunar surface here momentarily; we're configuring one of the cameras at the moment. With respect to the upward roll, it looks as though it's probably due mostly to the terrain. There's not really a good level spot to land on around here, unless we proceeded quite a bit closer to Doublet. So we'll keep you in, and we'll advise you further on that after we're had the EVA (Extravehicular Activity).

04-13-46-23 (McCandless)

Okay, very good. Sounds like you may have a nice level sight over near Doublet for the ALSEP though, doesn't it? [Note: The ALSEP was the Apollo Lunar Surface Experiments Package, which included a number of geophysical experiments.]

04-13-46-31 (Shepard)

Well, we'll find one.

04-13-50-03 (Shepard)

Okay, Houston, Antares here. You ready for some words on the surface?

04-13-50-08 (McCandless)

That's affirmative, Antares. Go ahead with your description.

04-13-50-22 (Shepard)
Okay. As you may have heard, after P64 at pitch-over, the Cone Crater and the landing site were immediately visible. The Sun-angle was good; we were able to recognize [the landing site] even easier than we were on the LNA display at the Cape. The LPD (Landing Point Designator) input are only one, and we took over short of a—of Triplet, and I thought at first I was going to land just south of the track, but it's rougher over there than the LNA shows. And so, we came back on track and landed. Since we held the track between Triplet and Doublet, and I estimate perhaps just 100 meters short of our target. Okay, with respect to the general terrain, we are in a depression here; we're looking, of course, directly toward Doublet Crater, which appears to be above us in elevation by approximately 25 to 30 feet. The terrain slopes gradually upward in that direction; there is—there are some modulations, but generally speaking it slopes gradually upward into the area of Doublet. The deactivated spacecraft is about one and a half degrees to the right of the landing plane, and of course that puts the shadow of the LM off to the left because of the current Sun location. Are you reading me, all right?

04-13-52-32 (McCandless)
That's affirmative, Antares; we're copying you 4-0. Over.

04-13-52-40 (Shepard)
Okay, while Ed is completing the pictures out of this window, I'll continue to say that generally speaking as I

sweep from one horizon to the other, we find that the terrain is a little rougher than I suspected, and we are in a depression here in the landing site with respect to the south and to the north. The depression at the north appears to be very close to us, approximately 50 or 60 meters away; to the south, the land gradually slopes up to a ridge, which is perhaps half a mile away. The general area in the left-hand window of the LM is relatively free of large boulders; I see less than 10 within my field of view that are—over the size of perhaps 8 to 10 inches. And now, Ed's ready to take over, and I'll proceed to photograph out the left window and turn it over to him.

04-13-54-01 (McCandless)
Roger, Ed. Go ahead.

04-13-54-04 (Edgar Mitchell: Lunar Module Pilot)
Okay, Houston. I'm just trying to get orientated; I think I can see quite a few of the craters that are out my window are here on the map. There are several large enough to be seen on the map, and in addition there's some reasonably large boulders. I will try to get us located first; then I'll describe what I see.

04-13-54-33 (McCandless)
Okay.

04-13-55-11 (Mitchell)
Well, it doesn't look like it's going to be quite easy, as easy as I thought, Houston, to pick out the craters that I see in front of me, and point, on the map until we get a little bit better; a clear view from the outside. Let

me just pick it up with a description. First of all, as Al pointed out, we're very close to the landing site that was proposed.

04-13-56-11 (McCandless)
Roger; and continue.

04-13-56-35 (Mitchell)
Okay, Houston. As Al pointed out, toward Doublet is a rise, and then the ridge that we had talked about that is beyond Doublet is very pronounced. It forms our skyline or my near horizon. And we seem to be sitting in a bowl. It slopes toward us from the west; it's rather choppy, I might admit, undulating, but the ridge beyond Doublet is the highest thing I can see in front of me. Looking around to the right, the—skyline is quite undulating. There is a large, old depression to our right or that—that is to the north of us, which forms another bowl very similar to the one that we are—appear to be sitting in. And I can see several ridges and rolling hills of perhaps 35 to 40 feet in height. Obviously very, very old craters that are almost lost—almost indistinct now between myself and the skyline to the north—the horizon to the north. It just looks like a series of low hills from this vantage point.

04-13-58-16 (Shepard)
Okay. And the window photography is completed. Magazine Kilo Kilo, exposure 20.

04-13-58-24 (McCandless)
Houston, Roger. Out.

04-13-58-27 (Mitchell)
Okay, Houston. The undulations are far too complex for me to try to describe them right now, without getting in a better vantage point so I can point them out on your map. I'm sure I can do that as soon as I can get a better handle on our location. Let me suffice it to say that I think there is more terrain, more relief here, than we anticipated from looking at the maps.

04-13-58-56 (Shepard)
There's a hell of a lot of relief inside the cabin, I'll tell you that.

04-13-59-05 (Mitchell)
Okay. And there's a few boulders out my window. They're scattered around falling between here and Doublet. I see at about my 2:30 position, probably 50 yards out, a large boulder that's probably 3 feet across. There—that's the largest one I have in my field of view, or at least, in my near field of view. And, there are two or three others perhaps half that size—or appear to be half that size in that same vicinity, Just a little, little beyond, about—about 2:30 on the clock code and perhaps 50 meters to the largest one and then another 10 or 15 to the other—the other big—boulders. They don't seem to form a pattern that I can see. The color that we're looking at is a kind of a mouse-brown or mouse-gray. And, obviously, it changes with the Sun angle. The surface—Well, there are craters in my field of view. Some old, very subdued, some overlapped by newer craters. Some that seem to be relatively recent.

Most of the surface, however, seems to be fine grain. Incidentally, I do see some linear features on the surface. Very small, fine linear features. I do not think that they are erosion patterns; they may be. However, I can see a suggestion of them quite a ways away from the LM, kind of running parallel to those that I can see, and we'll have to talk about later when we get out.

Getting Ready to Go Outside

Before we set foot on the Moon, there was still a lot of work to do inside the spacecraft. For the next five hours Alan and I read over all our checklists for what we were supposed to do next. This way we wouldn't waste precious time once we were walking on the Moon. We also made sure all our equipment and spacesuits were in top-notch condition. We then had a bite to eat. I know we were both famished and somehow all our plastic bags of freeze-dried food tasted better than ever.

Preparing to go outside in the tight fit of the Antares wasn't easy. We were already wearing our spacesuits, but it took a while to pull on everything else including our boots, gloves, helmets, and lunar backpacks. With our spacesuit plus the backpack, we weighed a whopping 400 pounds on Earth. But because the Moon has one-sixth the gravitational pull of Earth, we weighed only about 70 pounds now. These spacesuits and all their accoutrements were amazing technological designs that had to keep us alive in the harsh, airless environment of the Moon. Walking around the Moon was, in some ways, like being underwater on Earth. We needed to have a way to breathe as well as a way to protect our skin from the intense solar rays. Our spacesuits provided us with oxygen, kept us cool, and protected us.

Each layer of the suit had an important function. The layer closest to the body was a water-cooled nylon undergarment, the middle layer was made with neoprene to withstand the pressure of spaceflight, and the outer layer was made of white beta cloth to protect against scrapes, fire, heat, and any solar rays we might encounter.

Fortunately, we never felt too hot or cold in our spacesuits because we could regulate our own temperature. If we worked hard and started to sweat, for example, we could turn up the cooling system and cool down. Alan and I also wore large gloves with special rubber fingertips for handling our equipment and picking up Moon rocks.

A cloth cap was worn close to the head with earphones and a microphone so we could always communicate with each other and with Mission Control. A bubble Plexiglas helmet, which was attached to the neck ring of our spacesuit, went over the cap helmet. And last, a visor covered the Plexiglas helmet to protect us from the bright rays of the Sun. Inside the helmet a small tube enabled us to take sips of water. We'd just turn our heads and get a sip of water from a small bag of water inside our suit.

One of the most important parts of our spacesuit was the large, rectangular lunar backpack called a Portable Life Support System (PLSS). Without this piece of equipment we couldn't have survived even a few seconds on the Moon. The PLSS provided us with oxygen to breathe, electrical power for our radios, and temperature and humidity control. Most important, the backpack carried a maximum of five hours of oxygen for each of our Moonwalks.

I hate to think what might have happened if we'd gone over this five-hour time limit. But of course, we never did.

Stepping Out at Last

When Alan and I were fully suited up, it was hard not to laugh. It was like we were wearing not one but two bulky snowsuits so we could go out and play in the snow. But this time the "snow" on the Moon was a whole lot of lunar dust. And because it was hard to tell us apart in our white space-suits, Alan's suit had vivid red stripes on it.

After we got the okay from Mission Control, Alan was the designated man to head down the ladder to the Moon first. I followed him outside about four minutes later. A motion picture camera was mounted on the lower part of the Lunar Module to film us exiting the craft. The images were broad-cast back to Earth so people back home would have the oppor-tunity to see what we were doing.

When Alan stepped off the ladder and set foot on the Moon, his words were concise. "It's been a long way, but we're here." I knew Al had worked long and hard to get to this point, and it was an important and emotional moment.

Then it was my turn. I backed down the ladder, step by step, and heard the CAPCOM say, "Okay Ed, we can see you coming down the ladder now." I moved carefully but quickly.

"It's very great to be coming down," I replied. And then I jumped back past the last step of the ladder and landed on the surface.

I'd made it. I'd finally, finally made it.

The first thing I did was to figure out how to walk on the Moon, and I was curious to see what it would be like to get around in the reduced gravity. As I took one step and then another and another, I quickly realized I felt lighter on my feet, even in my stiff spacesuit. As I moved around in my new environment, I stepped over a few craters that were filled with dust. In some ways this reminded me of walking on a beach in Hawaii with its darker volcanic sand.

I looked over at the Antares and could easily see how one of the footpads had landed in a small crater. But it didn't seem to be a problem.

I then looked up at the sky. Boy did it look different. It was inky black without a star in sight and I couldn't see Earth at all. Alan and I later figured out that if we stood on the Antares ladder, hung onto the rails and leaned way back, we could see Earth, which was straight up above us and shaped like a crescent Moon.

But for a moment, I just wanted to stop, take in my surroundings, and stare at this amazing new place. And then I needed to get to work.

All the work we completed on the Moon was carefully thought out ahead of time, and Alan and I were responsible for the tasks of the original Apollo 13 mission that didn't make it to the Moon.

Our work was spelled out on checklists we wore on the wrist cuffs of our spacesuits. These checklists were detailed to-do lists that stated everything we were to accomplish from one moment to the next. With a checklist on one arm and a watch on the other, Alan and I were constantly looking at our wrists to stay on schedule and on task.

Time was a huge factor and there wasn't a moment to waste. We were always working against the clock, and both of us needed to stick to precise directions as to exactly what to do and when. We always had Mission Control talking to us through our earphones and asking us where we were, what we'd done, and if we were on schedule. We constantly heard, "You're two minutes behind. You're three minutes behind." This went on and on. Alan and I were so focused on getting all our work done that once we completed a task, we quickly moved on to something new.

WHERE ARE THE STARS?

When Alan and I worked on the Moon, we couldn't see any stars in the sky. This natural phenomenon happened because the sunlight was so bright during the lunar day, the stars were too dim compared to it, and thus not visible. The bright lunar sunlight caused the lenses of our eyes to shut down, as well as the lenses of our cameras.

This is the same phenomenon that occurs on Earth when we look up at the sky during the day and can't see any stars. The stars are out there, but because of the daylight brightness, we simply can't see them. We are able to see the stars in the Earth sky again when the sunlight becomes dimmer during nighttime.

All in a Day's Work

Our Moon work was scheduled over two days in two separate Moonwalks called ExtraVehicular Activities, or EVAs. Each EVA lasted about four and a half hours and, as mentioned, we had a five-hour oxygen limit in our backpack. Alan and I were always careful how long we worked on the Moon because we wanted to be back in the Antares before our oxygen and water ran out. At the end of each EVA, it took about 15 to 20 minutes to load all the Moon samples we collected into the Antares and climb back into the craft.

The two of us were constantly documenting and recording our lunar work with motion picture and still photography cameras. Alan and I had special cameras that were mounted on our spacesuits at chest level, which made it easier to take photos.

One of our first tasks was to remove the movie camera from the Lunar Module, where it had filmed us coming down the ladder. We then set it up on a tripod about 50 feet away from the craft. Here, the camera was in a good position to film the work we were about to do.

Next, I walked a few feet away from the craft and reached down to get a "contingency sample," which consisted of a few pounds of lunar surface material I collected and placed in a bag. We'd bring this sample back to Earth to analyze along with the many Moon rocks we would soon collect.

Another initial assignment was to set up the American flag, and we found a good spot to do this about 20 feet from the Antares. After Old Glory was standing tall on the Moon, it felt so surreal to think that Alan and I had just planted our flag way out in space on a distant, extraterrestrial land. The flag's bright red and white stripes, and its white stars against the navy blue fabric, looked so colorful against the gray backdrop of the Moon and the deep black sky.

Like lunar tourists, we then took each other's photo by the flag.

Mission Control let us know that US President Nixon had sent us a message saying he was watching the mission on his television at the White House and he wished us a good mission and safe trip home.

Our next task was to set up various pieces of scientific equipment including a circular S-band antenna, a solar-wind composition experiment, and a laser ranging retro-reflector. We worked fast and efficiently and got each of the jobs done.

Alan and I also assembled a hand-pulled cart called the MET, which was short for Modularized Equipment Transporter. The MET was the first wheeled vehicle used on the Moon and was designed to help us haul equipment and carry all the Moon rocks we'd collect during the mission. Later Apollo missions would use a vehicle called the Rover, which was an electric Moon buggy that could be driven across the lunar surface.

We then hiked nearly 650 feet to an area by the Doublet crater to set up a scientific package called the Apollo Lunar Surface Experiments Package (ALSEP), which included a number of scientific instruments and geophysical experiments. Alan pulled the MET, which hauled all the equipment, and I carried the heavy ALSEP in my hands like a barbell. It was a strenuous hike because of the rolling lunar terrain.

Once we were at our designated location, we set up the ALSEP, which remained on the Moon after we left and transmitted scientific data back to Earth.

Next, I set off a series of 13 small explosive charges called Thumpers. The Thumpers were seismic experiments to measure the upper part of the Moon's crust.

Even though Alan and I worked very hard, it seemed like we were always slightly behind our heavy workload, which was about 120 percent of human capacity.

NASA APOLLO 14 MISSION OBJECTIVES

The primary objectives of this mission were to explore the Fra Mauro region of the Moon with many scientific experiments including: deployment of the Apollo Lunar Surface Scientific Experiments Package (ALSEP); lunar field geology investigations; collection of surface material samples for return to Earth; deployment of other scientific instruments not part of ALSEP; orbital science involving high-resolution photography of candidate future landing sites; photography of deep-space phenomena, such as zodiacal light and Gegenschein; communications tests using S-band and VHF signals to determine reflective properties of the lunar surface; engineering and operational evaluation of hardware and techniques; tests to determine variations in S-band signals; and photography of surface details from 60 nautical miles in altitude.

Otherworldly Sleep

"Difficulties are just things to overcome, after all."

—Ernest Shackleton

After five hours of Moon work, Alan and I were ready to call it a day. Now exhausted, we made our way back to the Antares, climbed into the craft, and took off our helmets, gloves, and boots. We had dinner, standing up of course, and got ready for some shut-eye.

We slept in two hammocks that were suspended one on top of the other in a perpendicular "T" position, and I was in the lower hammock. Since it wasn't dark outside, we placed covers over the Lunar Module windows to block out the sunlight.

Alan and I talked about the day briefly, and we tried to fall asleep in this new and mysterious world. Even though we needed rest, it wasn't easy to sleep, especially since the Antares was tipped at an angle. After a few hours of restless sleep, we were startled awake by a disturbing noise.

"Did you hear that?" Alan said. He sounded alarmed.

"I sure did," I said.

We scrambled out of our hammocks and looked out the window to see what in the heck was going on. Had a small meteorite hit us? Was Antares was falling over? Was there something outside?

We didn't see anything suspicious out the window and the Antares seemed downright steady. So we decided we were fine. We got back into our hammocks and tried to sleep for the next few hours. This was our only rest period on the Moon and I doubt either of us got too much sleep. There was just too much to think about, and we couldn't wait to get outside again.

9

Trek to Cone Crater

"I had ambition not only to go farther than any one had been before, but as far as it was possible for man to go."
—*Captain James Cook*

"**W**ell, it's nice to be out in the sunny day again," I said as I climbed down the ladder of the Antares to greet Alan.

"Yes, it's a beautiful day here in Fra Mauro Base," Alan added.

It was day two of our Moon mission and we started our second EVA nearly two and a half hours early. We were glad to be outside again. Neither of us had gotten much sleep, but resting in our hammocks and having dinner and breakfast gave us new energy.

As I looked out at the lunar surface this second time, I was amazed at the intense contrast of light. The sun's rays cast long, stark shadows and everything looked very dark or very light. This looked so different from the softer colors of Earth.

Yet, in the Moon's bleakness, there was a peaceful stillness and calm.

And when I turned my eyes toward the heavens I caught another glimpse of the Moon's deep black, starless sky. It was mesmerizing. I wasn't able to see Earth at this point, but I certainly felt very connected to my world that was now so far away. Although Alan and I had prepared for many years to be able to walk on the Moon, it still felt exciting to be here. We'd already refilled our backpacks with oxygen and loaded the pouches in our spacesuits with fresh drinking water for the full day ahead. Our first EVA focused on observing our new world and setting up and conducting a number of science experiments. Today we were going on a geophysical traverse—in other words we were going to take a long hike. Our objective was to walk more than one mile to the large Cone Crater. As lunar explorers, we were going to use everything we'd learned in our geology training to find and collect Moon rocks that would help provide important clues about how the universe, the Moon, and even the Earth were once created long ago.

As the navigator on our trek to Cone Crater, I was responsible for tracking our journey. I carried a map to guide us during our traverse from the Lunar Module to Cone Crater and back to the Lunar Module again.

NASA geologists had selected designated points where Alan and I were instructed to collect lunar rock samples. A number of craters acted as visual landmarks along the way. We'd look for and pass by Triplet, Weird, Flank, Doublet, and of course, Cone. Each crater's name made sense. Three craters formed Triplet and there were two craters at Doublet. Flank Crater flanked Cone Crater, and Cone, as its name suggests, was large and cone-shaped. I guess the Weird Crater just looked unusual.

Each crater stop was called a "station" on the map and was designated with a letter. We started out at station A, and four and a half hours later we would end up at station H with a total of 15 stops.

We loaded the MET with our cameras and tools, and also carried an instrument called a Lunar Portable Magnetometer. This instrument could be taken on and off the MET, and we'd use it to measure the magnetic field of the Moon at two specific locations.

As we started our trek from the Antares, the surface of the Moon was relatively flat and not too rocky. The surface was, however, loaded with craters that we had to carefully step over and walk around. Alan and I both pulled the MET at different times, but in the beginning Alan pulled the cart while I followed him taking photos and collecting Moon rocks. The two wheels of the MET left very distinct tracks in the lunar dust, which I described to Mission Control. "The MET tracks make a very smooth pattern in the surface, reminiscent of driving a tractor through a plowed field," I said. "It smoothes it out and makes a very smooth, distinct pattern, and is probably a quarter of an inch deep, no more."

Even though it added more bulk to my spacesuit, I really enjoyed using my chest-mounted camera. I took many close-ups and long shots. Because it wouldn't have been easy to press a button on a camera with our thick Moon gloves, our cameras were designed with a trigger that could be pulled.

Whenever I wanted to take a photo, I'd simply point my camera at an object and pull the trigger.

As we got closer and closer to Cone Crater, the terrain became a lot more rugged and there were more rocks and boulders on our path. This made it harder to lug the MET along, and at times the cart would nearly tip over if we didn't hang on to it tightly.

A Rough, Challenging Hike

> "The surface of the Moon is not smooth, uniform, and precisely spherical as a great number of philosophers believe it to be, but is uneven, rough, and full of cavities and prominences, being not unlike the face of the Earth, relieved by chains of mountains and deep valleys."
>
> —Galileo Galilei

Although I was constantly looking at my map, it wasn't easy to judge distances on the Moon and our landmarks weren't always easy to find. One reason for this was because all the craters on the map were shown from a bird's-eye view taken from above in lunar orbit on earlier Apollo missions.

The craters looked very different at eye level. And it wasn't easy to tell one crater from another because the lunar surface often looked like a rolling sand dune and the edge of one crater often looked like the edge of another. We didn't want to get lost, so Alan and I would stand on top of a crater and look around so we knew exactly where we were. Fortunately, we did stay on our route the entire time.

But the work was stressful. We huffed and puffed as we walked, even in the reduced gravity of the Moon. It wasn't easy to lug along the MET or to walk across the rock-strewn surface. Our heart rates were continually monitored to make sure our bodies were not stressed from overexertion. Every once in a while, Mission Control would tell us to take a break because their monitors showed that our heart rates were too high.

Collecting Moon rocks was both an art and science. Like geologists on Earth, we often used special tools such as tongs to pick up rocks, or a geologist's hammer to chip off portions of rocks from larger lunar boulders. We placed all of our smaller rocks in plastic "Z bags" and loaded them into the MET.

The rocks came in different shapes, sizes, and formations, and most of them were made of lava. It's interesting to note that some of the rocks were white, some looked like glass, and others were formed with crystals. We also numbered the rocks and gave some of them names like Saddle Rock or Big Bertha. We were thrilled when we found Big Bertha; it was about the size of a football and the largest rock we brought back.

As the day wore on, our oxygen was becoming depleted and our heart rates were rising. Time was of the essence and Alan and I became very focused on getting to our destination: Cone Crater.

About 1,000 feet across and 800 feet deep, this enormous round crater was formed when a large meteorite impacted the Moon. The impact caused a great deal of material, or ejecta, to be thrown out and around the rim of the crater. The lunar rocks around the rim of Cone Crater would give us important clues about the Moon and Earth. But finding the rim of Cone Crater proved to be very difficult. The climb to the crater was getting steeper by the minute; Alan and I were finding it harder to breathe and our heart rates were starting to soar.

Mission Control asked us to turn back, but we didn't want to give up yet. We couldn't tell how close or far we were from Cone, and we needed more time.

"Okay, take 30 more minutes," CAPCOM Fred Haise told us.

So Alan and I kept plugging along. I was pulling the MET now, which became tougher to do as we hiked up Cone's steep incline. Alan helped me by picking up the other end of the cart. After 30 minutes, we could tell we were at the edge of Cone Crater because the area was overflowing with ejecta of rocks and boulders.

I talked with Mission Control and gave a highly detailed description of the edge of Cone Crater:

The area here is in an area of considerably more boulders, a larger boulder field, more numerous boulders than we've seen in the past. We've just come into it as we approached B from A. Now, there were boulders to the north of us; we previously talked of boulders to the north, and doggone it, they may turn out to be a ray pattern. It looks suspiciously like one. However, where we are now, we're about on the edge of a general boulder population lining the flank of Cone Crater. Now they're not too numerous at this point and are somewhat patchy. There's a lot of them buried, half buried, a few of the smaller ones sitting on the surface. These boulders are filleted, and we'll have to sample that filleting later. The surface texture—the fine—appears very much the same as what we've been walking on all along. And about the only difference we could see is probably a larger number of smaller craters. I say 'probably'; they're so numerous that unless you really make a population count, you can't tell. I'm guessing a larger number of craters—probably secondary's from Cone perhaps—and certainly a larger number of boulders lying around. Now, most of these boulders are rounded. There are a few angular ones. There are a few rocks with angularities; but, by and large, you can see edges that have been chipped off indicating the beginning of a smoothing process. And some of them are far beyond the beginning of smoothing; they're worn down pretty well. And most of the rough edges are where they have fractured and perhaps turned over. Most of them appear to be along fractures of where other rocks are sitting near them that might have once been a part of that boulder.

Alan and I then got to work collecting specimens and chipping off rock samples before loading them into the MET. The rocks were extremely hard and chipping off the pieces wasn't easy to do. Our extra 30 minutes had gone fast, and because we were getting even lower on oxygen, Mission Control finally told us that we had to turn back. There was no more negotiating for more time.

Unfortunately, Alan and I didn't get a chance to stand on the rim of Cone Crater and peer down into it, which we both really wanted to do. I imagine it would have been like looking over the edge of the Grand Canyon and seeing the magnificence of it all. Yes, it was disappointing. But most important, we'd made it to the edge of Cone Crater and we'd collected a huge haul of Moon rocks.

Alan and I then turned around and headed back to the Antares, collecting more lunar samples along the way. When we finally got back to the Lunar Module, there was still a bit of time to make history.

The First Lunar Olympics

Before leaving the Moon, Alan and I decided to have some fun and games. Using a piece of equipment from one of our science experiments, Alan creatively assembled a golf club with the head of a six iron he'd carried with him. We still had the camera going, so everything was filmed for the world to see—and enjoy.

"Houston . . . you might recognize what I have in my hand as the handle for the contingency sample return," Alan said to the camera. "It just so happens to have a genuine six iron on the bottom of it. In my left hand, I have a little white pellet that's familiar to millions of Americans. I'll drop it down."

Alan dropped a golf ball he'd been carrying in the pocket of his spacesuit into the lunar dust. "Unfortunately, the suit is so stiff, I can't do this with two hands," he added. "But I'm going to try a little sand-trap shot here." He took a one-handed shot and missed.

"You got more dirt than ball that time," I joked.

"Got more dirt than ball," Alan confessed. "Here we go again."

LUNAR RECORDS

On February 5 and 6, 1971, Alan Shepard and I were on the surface of the Moon for nearly 34 hours. We walked directly on the surface of the Moon for nine hours and 17 minutes and covered a distance of nearly five kilometers. We hold the record for having the longest Moonwalk on foot of all the Apollo missions.

Alan and I accomplished a great deal of scientific work such as observing the lunar surface, setting up a science station, conducting science experiments, and hiking over the lunar surface to collect nearly 100 pounds of Moon rocks and other lunar samples.

Alan finally whacked the ball, which went sailing into a crater about 50 feet away. "Straight as a die. Miles and miles and miles," Alan said as if he'd made a hole in one.

Not to be outdone, I then took out a thin rod from our solar wind experiment and used it as a javelin. I hurled my javelin through the vacuum of space and right toward the crater where Alan's golf ball had landed. "There's the greatest javelin throw of the century," Alan added.

It was great to see the rod zip away, and I've always been happy to say that my javelin landed a few inches farther than Alan's golf ball.

We packed up all our Moon rocks and equipment and started to load our bounty into the Lunar Module. This was another endeavor that required ingenuity. I climbed into the Antares, and the two of us used an innovative rope-and-pulley mechanism for loading. Alan would hook a plastic bag holding a rock onto the line and then send it up to me. It was a simple system but worked quite well.

Before climbing up the ladder and into the Antares for the very last time, I stopped and took one last look. I had the profound realization that I'd never be here again. I then held onto the rails and leaned way back, as far back as I could go. I looked straight up to catch one last glimpse of Earth, in its beautiful crescent shape.

What a beauty, I thought. *What a beauty.*

I crawled into the spacecraft and Alan followed shortly thereafter. Although it wasn't easy to leave, both of us were eager to see Stu again, and head back home.

LUNAR PLAQUES

Apollo Moon Missions 11, 12, 14, 15, 16, and 17 left honorary seven-by-nine-inch stainless steel plaques on the Moon. These plaques were attached to the landing gear of the lower part of the Lunar Modules and will remain on the Moon for all time. The first Apollo 11 Moon mission plaque was signed by astronauts Neil A. Armstrong, Michael Collins, Edwin E. Aldrin Jr., and Richard Nixon, President, United States of America. The plaque reads:

HERE MEN FROM THE PLANET EARTH
FIRST SET FOOT UPON THE MOON
JULY 1969, A.D.
WE CAME IN PEACE FOR ALL MANKIND

The Apollo 14 plaque was signed by astronauts Alan B. Shepard Jr., Stuart A. Roosa, and Edgar D. Mitchell, and reads:

APOLLO 14
ANTARES
FEBRUARY 1971

The Extraordinary Ride Home

> " . . . a dream that became a reality and spread through-
> out the stars"
>
> —*Captain Kirk, Star Trek*

Covered in a light layer of Moon dust, Alan and I stood at the controls of the Antares. We were busy reviewing our flight procedures and getting ready for lunar liftoff. Everything seemed in order.

But then an uncomfortable thought occurred to me. *What if ignition doesn't work?* I knew ignition failure was a remote possibility, but with any technology, problems can occur. We certainly didn't want to be stuck on the Moon because once our oxygen was depleted, our lives would end in a very short amount of time. We also knew that if something went wrong, we would be completely on our own because Stu wouldn't be able to fly the Kitty Hawk down here to get us.

Fortunately, there were plenty of backup procedures that Alan and I had trained for. We never wanted to be caught by surprise and not know how to handle a situation.

I looked at Alan and wondered if he was thinking the same thing. But neither of us said a word. And then, I was suddenly distracted by the loud voice of the CAPCOM. "We're coming up now on 10 minutes until lunar liftoff." I was glad to hear his words.

Think positive, I thought. In 10 minutes we'd be lifting off from the Moon and heading toward Stu. In my mind's eye I could see myself sitting in the Command Module again, and that was reassuring.

"Antares, Houston. We're coming up on four minutes," Mission Control said. "Stand by. Mark four minutes." The minutes passed quickly.

"Okay, the abort stage is set and the ascent engine is armed," Alan said. "Six, five, four, three, two, one . . ."

"Ignition!" I called out.

Our ascent engine powered up just as it was supposed to. *Great. Excellent,* I thought.

I could feel a powerful surge and a jolt as the upper "ascent" half of the Antares lifted up and separated from the bottom "descent" half of the craft that was now playing a crucial role as our launch pad. Our craft started to rise up, up, and away from the Moon, and we would slowly and gradually pitch over from a vertical position to a horizontal one as we approached Stu's orbital altitude.

"What a liftoff," I said. I felt partly relieved, but mostly thrilled.

We then began a critical procedure called a "direct rendezvous trajectory" that flew us directly up to Stu. Stu was flying the Kitty Hawk around the Moon in the higher orbit above the lunar surface. Once we were in Stu's orbit, we would then fly right behind him and eventually reconnect the Antares with the Kitty Hawk. That is, if everything went as planned.

Our primary goals at this point were to fly up to Stu, reconnect our two spacecraft, and head back to Earth. Of course, Mission Control, Alan, Stu, and I all had one overriding concern—would the Antares be able to dock with the Kitty Hawk? We'd had so much trouble docking six days earlier and we absolutely couldn't afford this problem now. We knew we had to make this procedure work. Stu was our ride home.

As our two spaceships got closer, Stu spotted us and it was obvious he was happy about it. "What are you doing way down there, oh fearless ones?" he joked. "You've lost a little weight since the last time I saw you."

Stu had a fun-loving sense of humor and we got a big kick out of his antics. He was making light of the fact that we had left the lower part of the Antares on the Moon after it completed its job as our launching pad.

Alan and I could also see the Kitty Hawk out our window as we approached it. "Oh, you look good," Alan said.

Then, when we were very close to the Kitty Hawk, Stu rotated the entire craft in a large 360-degree loop so Alan and I could inspect it for any telltale signs of trouble.

"And around we go," Stu said.

"That's our home away from home," I added. It was so great to see the Kitty Hawk up close again. Alan and I didn't see any problems with the craft.

Then we heard Mission Control give us the go-ahead.

"Apollo 14, this is Houston. You're go for the docking."

Slowly and very smoothly, the Antares matched speeds and moved in to dock with the Kitty Hawk. We held our breath and hoped for the best.

Then with a snap, snap, and a few clicks, we connected.

"Okay, we capture," I said loudly and clearly.

This time, we didn't need to try and try again; we connected right away. However, in the event we couldn't connect, we did have an extravehicular maneuver where Alan and I would have crawled outside the Lunar Module in space, then crawled inside the Command Module. But this was an extremely dangerous backup plan, and we were glad we didn't need to use it.

"Beautiful," the CAPCOM replied. "There's a big sigh of relief being breathed around here."

"And all over the world," Stu added.

Knock, Knock

Still covered in dust, Alan and I looked a bit like cowboys coming home after a long, hard day on the range. We knew Stu wouldn't be thrilled about it; he'd been living alone in the spotless and sanitary Command Module for the past few days. But Alan and I couldn't wait to crawl back into the Kitty Hawk. Alan got right up to the Lunar Module hatch and knocked a few times to let Stu know we were ready to come in.

"Who's there?" Stu joked.

Stu then opened the door and we climbed in. Without wasting even a minute, we cleaned off as best we could. We then took off our bulky spacesuits and put on our lightweight coveralls. What a relief that was.

But it wasn't quite time to sit back and relax. For the next hour or so, Alan, Stu, and I worked hard to transfer all of our rock samples, cameras, and experimental data from the Lunar Module to the Command Module.

When this work was done, we shut and locked the hatch for one last time. We said good-bye to our trusty, bug-like Antares, which we then jettisoned to crash back on the Moon to create a small "Moonquake." The Antares was never designed to return to Earth, but it played an important role until its very end. Once the Antares crashed at a predetermined location on the Moon, the seismic signals were picked up by the seismometer Alan and I had placed on the lunar surface, as well as a seismometer that had been left by the Apollo 12 astronauts. This data provided more information about the interior structure of the Moon.

Alan and I took our seats again in the Command Module and buckled ourselves in. Now it was time to head back to Earth. I was sure looking forward to a home-cooked meal with my family, and I knew there'd be many great stories to share. But we needed a big boost to send us on our way. When we were on the far side of the Moon again, our engines ignited in a "trans-Earth injection" sequence. This thrust gave us plenty of power to blast us all the way home.

Last Leg of the Journey

After a few hours of work, and a dinner of ham and potatoes in a bag and eight ounces of grapefruit juice, my sleep hammock was starting to look very inviting. I was tired to the bone and anxious to get some rest. Alan and I both needed sleep and were able to nod off in no time at all.

The next morning Mission Control woke us up. "How are you all this morning?" The CAPCOM sounded chipper as ever.

"Really great, really great." I said. "How are things there?"

"Beautiful. Everybody's relaxed down here and anticipating your arrival on schedule."

Alan, Stu, and I felt the same. We had worked very hard on our lunar mission and accomplished what we set out to do. We were all in good spirits.

The Kitty Hawk stayed on its steady course and moved along at a speed that increased from about 3,500 feet per second to 6,500 feet per second. This is fast considering that there are 5,280 feet per mile. At times we were traveling nearly one mile per second.

At this point in the journey everyone's duties were lighter and we were all unwinding. It felt great. I started to reflect on everything I had just experienced over the last six days. I thought about our launch and the thunderstorm delay. I recalled the many frustrating attempts we had made trying to dock our spacecraft at the start of the mission. I remembered the scare with the abort light and radar during our lunar landing. And of course I replayed every moment of our two Moonwalks: walking around the alien lunar surface, setting up and conducting the science experiments, and hiking toward Cone Crater.

There were thousands of things to think about. But what I remembered most was the first time I set eyes on Earth from deep space on our way to the Moon. It was a powerful experience and a beautiful sight to behold.

In preparation for our return, Mission Control gave us an update on current events. We heard about an earthquake near the Aleutian Islands of Alaska. We found out that a radio station in Moberly, Missouri, had tried to place a prank phone call to talk with us when we were on the Moon. And we learned that Golden Globe Awards went to actor George C. Scott for his lead role in the movie *Patton* and to Ali MacGraw for her lead role in the movie *Love Story*.

Sometimes Mission Control would play us tunes from films such as *Camelot*. We even had a deep-space news conference while flying home. Mission Control linked us in with reporters who asked detailed questions about our mission and Moonwalks. I thought this was an interesting aspect of our work. When we were about halfway home, we heard that someone had sent a bouquet of red roses to Mission Control on behalf of our return to Earth.

What in the World?

The ride home was absolutely remarkable and I'll never forget it.

On two of the nights, I conducted two more of my ESP experiments as I had planned. But during the day, when I had more time to sit back and relax, I enjoyed peering out my window and taking in the sights. I truly felt like a cosmic sightseer.

And then something extraordinary happened to me.

As our spacecraft headed toward Earth, it was constantly rotating in the barbecue mode as it had done on the way to the Moon. These slow rotations protected the craft, but they also gave me a spectacular view. As we turned, I was able to see a breathtaking 360-degree panorama of the heavens with the Earth, the Moon, the Sun, and the many glistening stars passing by the window. And because there's no atmosphere in space, everything looked 10 times brighter than on Earth. It was a fantastic sight—I knew I had a ringside seat to one of the greatest shows of the universe. Pretty soon I was hooked and couldn't take my eyes off the view. And then, all at once, a wonderful feeling washed over me from head to toe. It was an amazing, joyful sensation, and I guess you could say it was *out of this world.*

On top of all the good feelings I was experiencing, I suddenly had a moment of deep insight. It was an overwhelming realization that my body and mind were connected to everything in the universe. I felt a deep, deep connection with all of life and a sense of oneness with the cosmos.

I knew Stu was asleep, but I wondered if Alan was also feeling what I was feeling. I looked over at him and could see he was busy talking with Mission Control. He didn't appear to be experiencing anything out of the ordinary.

Confused and a bit stunned, I tried to intellectually make sense of what was happening. I knew from my studies in astronomy that all matter in the universe was originally created in ancient star systems. And right now I was keenly aware that the molecules of my body, as well as the molecules of Alan and Stu's bodies, and even the molecules of our spacecraft, were also created in these ancient star systems.

It was a profound and ecstatic realization. First of all, I realized I was connected to the universe, and second, I realized there was a unity to everything and everyone.

To my delight, this naturally good feeling lasted for the next three days on our return to Earth. All I needed to do was look out my window and stare at the brilliant stars against the deep black sky—and there was that wonderful feeling again.

Of course, I was naturally flooded with questions. *What in the heck is happening to me? Why do I feel this way? What in the world is going on?*

The Shock of Reentry

The Kitty Hawk was right on track in terms of its velocity and trajectory toward Earth. As our spacecraft got closer to our planet's gravitational field, our speed got faster and faster.

Our landing site was near the Samoan Islands, which are located way out in the middle of the South Pacific Ocean. The closest town to our landing was Pago Pago (the capital of American Samoa), and it was nearly 900 miles away.

I knew there was going to be discomfort on reentering Earth's atmosphere, and I knew the plummet into the South Pacific would be abrupt. But we couldn't get back home without this fiery, difficult, and dangerous part of the ride.

When we were about four hours from splashdown, we were traveling about 11,000 feet per second, or nearly two miles per second. One hour before reentry, we moved even faster at a speed of nearly 20,000 feet per second.

I was glad when we heard from Mission Control.

"Apollo 14, this is Houston. All your systems are looking good from down here and we're in great shape for the entry."

That was great news to me. "Everything looks good from up here," I said.

The large USS *New Orleans* aircraft carrier was already about five miles from our landing site and waiting for us.

And there were recovery helicopters and navy frogmen set to retrieve us.

We got closer and closer and closer to Earth.

About 15 minutes before reentry, we had to complete two important procedures. First, we jettisoned the Service Module, which burned up and dropped into the ocean. Next, we needed to turn our Command Module around so that the widest part of the craft was facing the ocean. We were about to enter a fiery zone, and to protect us from the intense heat of reentering Earth's atmosphere, our Command Module was built with a specially designed heat shield on its wide base. This heat shield was several inches thick and made of a tough resin that would melt and burn off during reentry. We depended on this heat shield for our lives; temperatures on the outside of the Kitty Hawk could get up to 5,000 degree Fahrenheit, which is hot enough to melt metals. All this heat would be generated from the friction of moving from the absence of atmosphere in space to the dense atmosphere of Earth.

Once our Command Module had turned around as it was supposed to, our backs (and not our fronts) now faced the Earth. This meant that we were looking out at space versus looking down at Earth as we returned home. In a manner of speaking, we were truly going "back to Earth."

Then, with only 24 seconds left, we were bulleting toward Earth at the mind-blowing speed of 36,000 feet per second. We were literally traveling about seven miles per second!

Next on the checklist? A complete communication blackout with Earth, which would last about three and a half minutes. There was no way around it—we would need to endure this blackout once we slammed into Earth's atmosphere.

But were we ready? Could we do it?

Thankfully, Mission Control was in contact with us at this critical time. "Apollo 14," the CAPCOM said with a calm, reassuring voice. "It's about eight seconds to the blackout. We'll talk to you when you come out the other side. Over."

"Okay, sounds good," Alan replied.

We braced ourselves, and then—BAM!

Hurtling into Earth's atmosphere was incredibly strong and powerful, like the wallop of a lifetime. I felt pressed against the back of my couch because the pressure was intense. Without a moment to catch our breaths, we were in the fiery three-minute inferno traveling on the most intense ride of our lives.

As the Kitty Hawk zoomed to Earth, it seemed to burst into colorful flames. Out of the corner of my eye I could see red-hot orange globules shooting past my window. Logically, I knew this was the resin melting off the heat shield, but at the time it just looked fiery.

The three and a half minutes seemed to take a heck of a lot longer than normal. But, eventually it passed, and we got through it.

Mission Control was right there when we emerged from the blackout. "Apollo 14! Apollo 14! This is Houston. How do you read? Over."

"Pretty good here," Stu answered. He didn't say much; we were all feeling like we'd been on the most dynamic roller coaster of all time.

Now, at 10,000 feet above Earth, our pace slowed down dramatically when three enormous red-and-white-striped parachutes opened. I could feel the sensation of gravity now more than ever before. Having been in space for so many days, it felt unusual to go from zero G to seven Gs in just a few seconds. The tug of gravity was a reminder I was home, and I became more aware of the heaviness of my body as our capsule slowly drifted down and floated toward our landing site. And then we smacked into the Pacific waters with a forceful thud.

Splashdown! We had returned to our watery Blue Planet.

Deadly Lunar Bugs?

Alan, Stu, and I prepared to exit the spacecraft. Out in the ocean, navy frogmen were speed swimming toward our Command Module, which had cooled down after plunging into the water. After the swimmers reached us, they tied a large life raft to the side of the spacecraft and waited for us to open the hatch. I admired the navy swimmers because they were the first humans to come into contact with us after our return from the Moon. At this point, the swimmers had no idea what they might be exposed to; they took a risk in rescuing us.

There were many unknowns with the first few Moon missions. Scientists were never sure what dangerous bugs we might bring back on our clothes, in our bodies, or in the rocks and equipment that returned. So, once we opened the hatch, three biological breathing masks and three biological coveralls were thrown to us. We put on the protective clothing and climbed out of the Kitty Hawk and into the raft. Each one of us then stepped into a wire basket to be hoisted up into the air and into a helicopter hovering over the water. Once we were on the helicopter, we were flown to the USS *New Orleans*, where many sailors were waving their arms to greet us and a small military band was playing.

THE EXTRA-TERRESTRIAL EXPOSURE LAW

In 1969 when the Apollo 11 crew first traveled to the Moon, the United States enforced Title 14, Section 1211 of the Code of Federal Regulations. This law, more commonly known as the Extra-Terrestrial Exposure Law, was passed on July 16, 1969, to prevent Earth and its inhabitants from any kind of biological contamination that might be brought back from space to Earth by astronauts as well as by their spacecraft, equipment, and/or lunar samples. Originally the law required the Apollo astronauts to be quarantined upon return to Earth for a specific period of time, but NASA stopped enforcing the quarantine regulation after the Apollo 14 mission; it was determined that the astronauts and the lunar materials were not a hazard to humans, animals, or plants. The law stayed in effect until 1991 when it was formally removed from the Code of Federal Regulations.

It was an exciting but unusual time. Being on Earth again was strange. My body wasn't used to Earth's gravity and I felt light-headed and heavy. Something as familiar as taking a step to walk now took concentration. I didn't feel like myself at first. I wanted to fill my lungs with the salty ocean air instead of breathing through my tight-fitting mask.

More Bug Barricades

Our new home aboard the USS *New Orleans* was a tightly sealed mobile home called the Mobile Quarantine Facility, or MQF. Inside the MQF, we were allowed to take off our masks and coveralls and enjoy a hot shower for the first time in nine days. A doctor gave each of us a medical exam to make sure we were okay, and then we sat down to a delicious meal of steak and potatoes.

The Command Module was also brought aboard the USS *New Orleans*. In just a few hours the entire MQF, with us in it, was lifted into a large cargo plane. We were soon flying back to the Manned Spacecraft Center in Houston.

Our next and last quarantined home was called the Lunar Receiving Laboratory at the Manned Spacecraft Center, where we would stay for about three weeks.

11

Expanding Horizons

"Do not go where the path may lead,
go instead where there is no path and leave a trail."
—*Ralph Waldo Emerson*

Being in quarantine for a second time was harder than ever. I'd been away for nearly one month and I missed my family. I wanted to go outside, breathe the fresh air, and get some exercise. But rules are rules.

Alan, Stu, and I ate, slept, and worked under tightly sealed biological conditions in the Lunar Receiving Lab. We also made sure we didn't transmit any otherworldly germs or bugs to anyone or anything. Louise and the girls came to visit me, and we talked through a glass window as we'd done during my first quarantine at the Kennedy Space Center before liftoff. It was fantastic to see everyone again, and I'm sure they were relieved to see I was safe and sound.

On a daily basis, Alan, Stu, and I were subjected to all sorts of medical examinations by medical staff hidden behind white masks, caps, and biological coveralls. It was a surreal setting and I went along with the program. But to be honest, I never felt worried about any kind of lunar contamination.

Scientists also kept a close watch on a litter of mice. These mice had been born and raised in highly sterile conditions and lived with us in the lab. The scientists thought that if the mice suddenly became ill, this might be a sign of some form of unusual contamination. Fortunately, all the critters remained healthy.

After three weeks, Alan, Stu, and I showed no signs of illness or contamination, and it was eventually determined there wasn't a Moon bug in sight. NASA also concluded that Moon contamination was not a threat to our planet. Apollo 14 was the last lunar mission to quarantine astronauts after their return to Earth, and I'm sure future Apollo astronauts were grateful for this.

The Science of Moon Rocks

For now, the three of us remained in the lab and we had a lot to do. One of my first projects was to work with Alan to sort out, label, weigh, photograph, and write reports about the many Moon rocks and lunar samples we'd brought back. These rocks provided important keys to help geologists and scientists figure out the Moon's history and how it was formed. They also provided a unique way to learn about Earth and the cosmos.

Sometimes I would hold the Moon rocks and just stare at them. I knew the rocks were billions of years old, and it was amazing to think Alan and I had collected these ancient specimens.

Eventually, the lunar rocks were distributed to more than 185 scientific teams in the United States and to 14 other countries. The rocks were carefully cut into thin, translucent sections and studied under a microscope. These microscopic sections often revealed rich geometric patterns of blues, greens, reds, yellows, oranges, and black.

Going Home

After 21 days in the Lunar Receiving Lab, Alan, Stu, and I were released to return to our homes. But it wasn't long before a new part of our adventure began: being a Space Age celebrity. People were curious about what had happened while we were on the Moon, and they wanted to honor our achievements. Our lives became filled with parties, parades, news conferences, and gala events.

On March 1, 1971, Alan, Stu, and I, and our wives, were invited to the White House for a formal dinner with President Nixon and his wife, Pat. The president awarded us NASA's Distinguished Service Medal, and in a moment of levity, he gave Alan a plaque titled the "Distinguished Order of Lunar Duffers," in honor of his famous Moon golfing. It was all in good fun.

The three of us were often in the spotlight; it seemed like we were always being interviewed for television, the radio, or the press. I wasn't used to all this attention, but we wanted to get the word out about the exciting Apollo 14 mission.

Big Changes Ahead

After coming back from the Moon I knew I would never be the same again. I felt like a changed man. I had grown and expanded in so many ways, and I was sure my life was about to lead in a whole new direction.

One of the first things I did after returning to Earth was to contact the two doctors and two psychics who had participated in my deep-space ESP experiments. I was very eager to compare notes.

It was exciting to learn that we had all written down a significant amount of similar numbers and symbols at the same time even though we were thousands of miles apart. The experiment persuaded me that ESP could happen, and these results were later published in a scientific journal. I also learned that the results of our ESP experiment were similar to those of science experiments on Earth that had already shown telepathy was a real possibility. But most important, my deep-space ESP experiment had planted a life-changing seed in my mind about how the mind works, and I wanted to learn a lot more about human consciousness.

A Million Questions

I was also extremely curious to figure out what had happened to me during the ride home in the Command Module. It was an extraordinary experience and I had a burning desire to learn more. I talked with a number of other astronauts and learned that they had also experienced similar feelings during their missions in space.

OUR PERSONAL PREFERENCE KITS

Most of us like to take personal items with us when we travel. Even astronauts. NASA allowed astronauts to bring along personal items and mementos in small beta cloth bags called Personal Preference Kits, or PPKs. On the Apollo 14 mission, Alan brought along his famous golf balls in his PPK, and I brought along a small chart for my ESP experiments and a set of microfilm cards of the *King James Bible*, on behalf of Reverend John M. Stout, director of the Apollo Prayer League. Two previous missions, Apollo 12 and Apollo 13, had tried to land the Bible on the Moon, and we were finally able to do so during Apollo 14.

Stu Roosa brought along hundreds of tiny redwood, loblolly pine, sycamore, Douglas fir, and sweet gum tree seeds. Stu had a love of trees and the outdoors, and before becoming an astronaut he worked for the US Forest Service as a smoke jumper. Stu would parachute out of airplanes to fight forest fires that were raging in areas that were difficult to reach. During Apollo 14, he was curious how his tree seeds would fare in space and if they would grow normally once planted back on our planet. After returning to Earth, Stu's many Moon Tree seeds were germinated in labs for nearly four years and then planted all over the world. These trees serve as long-lasting and living reminders of the courageous astronauts who ventured to the Moon.

I began to read and read and read. I wanted to get my hands on anything that would help me understand what happened to me while peering out the Command Module window, and I felt compelled to unravel this cosmic mystery. I started to question what I'd learned in my science classes and especially in quantum physics. I wondered if there was more to life than I'd ever expected, and whether the world as I'd known it wasn't quite as it appeared.

At first I talked with scientists and asked them about my experience. But when I didn't get answers that I felt explained what I had experienced, I turned to people who studied in different fields such as religion, spirituality, and mysticism. Suddenly I wanted to know a lot more about the cosmos, the origins of creation, human beings, and consciousness.

One idea that caught my attention was a concept called "metanoia." *Metanoia* is an ancient Greek word that means a change of mind or a change of heart, and it relates to the concept of transformation. I finally realized that this was what I had experienced in my spacecraft coming home. I had actually felt a transformative change of heart and mind.

I also discovered that many mystical traditions have similar words for metanoia. For example, in Zen Buddhism the word *satori* describes what happens when someone has a sudden spiritual awakening and enlightenment. In Hinduism, the Sanskrit word *samadhi* describes a sudden awakened state of consciousness. In the West, some individuals call this experience the "ecstasy of unity," which is a shift in consciousness and a shift in awareness.

New Beginnings

In 1972, about one year after I returned from the Moon, I decided to retire from a 20-year career in the navy where I had achieved the rank of captain. I also decided to retire from NASA and the Astronaut Corps. I was 42 years old and felt like I had a whole new life ahead of me. I realized that after my Apollo 14 journey, I had gone from "outer space to inner space" in a matter of months, and I now wanted to devote the rest of my life to the exploration of the mind.

Louise wasn't thrilled with my new direction. For many years she had been very patient and supportive of my career. She'd already been through a lot of changes while I was in the navy, and the demanding schedule of my work as an astronaut was intense. Suddenly I was very excited about a whole new career path studying the mind, and Louise found this difficult to accept. Sadly, we began to part ways.

But I felt compelled to pursue this new direction and couldn't wait to get started. In 1973, two years after I returned from the Moon, I founded the Institute of Noetic Sciences (IONS). The word *noetic* comes from the ancient Greek word *nous*, which refers to an intuitive and expanded consciousness, and a person's inner knowing. The institute was first briefly located in Houston, and then it moved from Palo Alto to Sausalito, California, before finally moving to the current location near Petaluma, California.

The metanoia I'd had in space was life changing. It occurred to me that if this experience happened to many people around the world, science could investigate and document things such as a metanoia, satori, samadhi, or ecstasy of unity. So, with the help of many dedicated individuals, IONS became dedicated to advancing our understanding of science, consciousness, and the human experience. Many new frontiers have been explored, such as the bridge between science and spirituality, the healing arts, consciousness, and human behaviors such as love, forgiveness, gratitude, and compassion. For nearly 40 years, many individuals have worked with IONS to help humans learn to love one another by knowing that we're all in this together and that we're all one. This is the noetic message, and it's what transformation and enlightenment are all about.

Our Incredible Spaceship Earth

Many astronauts have said that if our world leaders could see Earth from deep space, we would have completely different political and economic systems on this planet. I agree. Going to the Moon helped me appreciate the magnificence of our world. When I could see Earth through the window of the Kitty Hawk or while standing on the Moon, I suddenly saw our planet in a whole new light. I could see how incredibly beautiful our blue-green Earth looked against the black sky. It was my home.

I suddenly felt very protective of Earth and started to see everything on the planet in a more sacred way. Even though I had been in the military, I now felt a strong aversion to war and I became a peacenik. I also started to learn about the practice of meditation, which is a way to quiet the mind and focus one's thoughts inward. I still practice meditation today and it helps me reduce negative thoughts as well as have inspirational ideas.

I even began to rethink the foods I eat. As a farm boy, I learned firsthand about where our food comes from. But my experience of going to the Moon and back expanded my way of thinking to include a greater appreciation of the foods I consume.

I'm encouraged that many people today are rethinking everything from what we eat, to where we live, to how we get around, and to how we treat others. Scientists, engineers, and many individuals are working hard to create a healthier, more sustainable world with cleaner air, cleaner water, and new sources of cleaner, alternative energy such as wind or solar power.

Futurist and writer Buckminster Fuller made an important point when he said that Earth is like a gigantic spaceship and we, as humans, are like the crew. Fuller encouraged people to find ways to get along on our very special "Spaceship Earth."

Earth is a spectacular place and I feel fortunate to live here. I believe that each one of us is connected to all of life on this planet, as well as throughout the universe. It's my hope that "peace on Earth" isn't simply wishful thinking but will be a reality one day.

Exploring New Worlds

> "Two roads diverged in a wood, and I—I took the one less
> traveled by,
> and that has made all the difference."
>
> —Robert Frost

After I graduated from Carnegie Tech in 1952, I had looked forward to finding work in the growing field of industrial management. But instead my life took a new turn, and I eventually became a modern-day space explorer. It has made all the difference.

Being an explorer is part of who I am because I come from a family of pioneers. Nearly 150 years ago, my great-grandparents traveled from the state of Georgia to Texas in search of a better life. With only their simple belongings and a few head of cattle, they forged across hundreds of miles of wilderness in covered wagons. They courageously braved harsh weather, difficult terrain, and the constant threat of danger with the hope of finding fertile land, clean water, nutritious food, a favorable climate, and a friendly community to earn a living and raise a family.

But getting there wasn't easy, and each new day brought challenging unknowns. I'm sure they wondered, *Will we be safe? What will the weather be like? What will we encounter along the way? Will there be enough food and water?*

It's not easy to be a pioneer. It takes the willingness to tackle the unknown and the courage to risk one's life. Yet the exploration of Earth's land, waterways, and skies, and even of space, has been so important in our changing world. When American explorers Meriwether Lewis and William Clark set out in canoes in 1804, they traveled nearly 7,500 miles of uncharted territory from the Midwest region of the United States to the Pacific Northeast. At the time both men were young, skilled frontiersmen: Lewis was a captain in the army, and Clark was a former commanding officer. The two men were good friends, and their willingness to explore the unknown was enormously beneficial to the future growth and success of this country.

Evolving Perspectives

As humans have observed and explored this planet, different theories have been developed to explain the basic shape of our world and its place in the universe.

In ancient times it was thought that the world was a flat disc and not a round orb. People came to this conclusion when they looked out at the horizon. They observed that the distant land looked flat and would seem to drop off at the horizon. At the time this seemed to be a logical conclusion—the Earth looked flat, so it must be flat.

Many people also believed, long ago, that the Earth was the center of the universe and the other celestial bodies orbited around it. As people looked up at the sky, it logically appeared that the Sun, the Moon, the planets, and the stars revolved around the Earth on a daily basis. In astronomy this theory is called the "geocentric model," and it was a predominant theory in ancient Greece.

For centuries, people continued to believe that the Earth was flat and was the center of the universe. But with the exploration and discoveries of well-known astronomers such as Nicolaus Copernicus, Johannes Kepler, and Galileo Galilei, these concepts began to change.

Copernicus was the first person to say that the Sun is at the center of the universe and the Earth and the other celestial bodies orbit around it. This theory, called the "heliocentric model," was a revolutionary idea at the time. Many years later, Galileo and Kepler also studied the heavens and agreed that the Sun, and not the Earth, was the center of the universe. But people didn't believe them or Copernicus at first.

New and different ideas often challenge our core beliefs and can take a long time to accept. Many people who lived during the times of Copernicus, or Galileo and Kepler, refused to believe what these astronomers said about our world and called their ideas "patently absurd," "far-fetched," "blasphemous," or even "crazy."

Are We Alone?

Over time, our understanding of Earth and its place in the universe has changed. We no longer believe that the Earth is flat or that Earth is the center of the universe. But we still face challenging unknowns such as, "Are we alone in the universe?" and "Does life exist beyond Earth?"

Many people today, including scientists, astronomers, astronauts, and educators, believe that we are not the only conscious and intelligent beings in the universe. I also hold this point of view and believe that our vast cosmos is teeming with life. As we continue to look up and explore space, large telescopes like the Hubble Space Telescope and the Kepler Telescope are helping us see the universe in a whole new way. These telescopes show us a more vast, varied, and expansive cosmos than ever imagined. And it's very exciting.

The scientists who study images from the Hubble and Kepler telescopes are continually finding new planets with Earth-like environments. These newly discovered planets may be harbingers of life as we know it. And, these amazing new discoveries are helping us rethink who we are as humans.

Many people also wonder if we are, or have ever been, visited by intelligent beings who live beyond Earth. People question how a spaceship could travel vast distances and light years to get to, or land on, our planet. These ideas challenge how we think about reality, and they're not easy to comprehend or to explain scientifically.

I've been curious about extraterrestrials since I was a teen when I read in the local paper about the so-called flying saucer that crashed on a ranch near Roswell, New Mexico, in 1947. Although I didn't give the event a lot of thought at the time, I'm sure the Roswell incident ignited my curiosity about ETs and was part of the reason I became a space explorer. Over time I have come to accept the idea that there is life beyond Earth, and I feel very comfortable with this belief.

But whether you believe in life beyond Earth or not, there's no escaping the many images and stories about UFOs, spaceships, and ETs in our everyday world. Our world is flooded with these images in books, magazines, newspapers, movies, TV shows, the Internet, and even everyday items such as breakfast cereal packaging. They're part of modern cultures and they can affect one's personal views and how one feels.

Although there have been a number of benevolent ETs featured in movies such as *ET the Extra-Terrestrial, Starman,* or *Avatar,* it certainly seems like many of the ETs depicted in movies are negative and frightening. It's natural to wonder if intelligent life forms outside of Earth could be either threatening or kind to us.

How we regard life is always a matter of our own individual perspective, but I believe we have no reason to be afraid. Staying positive and loving in our lives is the key.

The Future of Space Exploration

Throughout my life I've had an ongoing desire to uncover the great unknowns and to shed light on some of the most basic questions we all face, such as *Who am I? Why am I here?* and *What's the purpose of my life?*

A great deal of my work as an explorer, scientist, astronaut, researcher, and educator has been to help unravel the many mysteries about our planet, the universe, and what it means to be human.

We learn through exploration, and exploration of any kind can challenge belief systems. It requires an open mind and a willingness to ask questions. I view the frontier of space as an ongoing, expansive vista for future exploration. Change is inevitable, and it's exciting to think about all the new discoveries awaiting us on this vast horizon.

Even in the last 100 years, our world has changed so much. My father was born about the time Orville and Wilbur Wright flew the world's very first airplane in 1903. And just 68 years later, I flew 240,000 miles to the Moon and walked on it. Now that's remarkable.

My great-grandparents would have found it impossible to believe that their great-grandson would one day walk on the Moon. They might have said, "Oh—that's a crazy idea!" They would have also found it nearly impossible to imagine inventions such as the television, microwave, computer, or smartphone.

And although we've seen big changes in the US space program, like the retirement of the NASA shuttle fleet, there will always be the continued exploration of our universe. There will be new and innovative space exploration in ways we can't even imagine, and I believe we must continue to be a space-faring civilization and always reach for the stars.

NASA continues to be a pioneer in space exploration and discovery. In 2011 NASA announced information about the design and development of a space launch system that could send astronauts even farther into space. Right now work is being done to design new spacecraft for long voyages that could send astronauts to an asteroid by 2025, and even to Mars by the mid-2030s, and return them safely to Earth. These are challenging long-range goals in the making, and some of our best thinkers are hard at work on these new expeditions into deep space.

As we begin this new era in space exploration, we will continue to find innovative avenues to head out into space. New changes in astronautics include moving toward space flight that is conducted through commercial and private companies versus the government. This will enable a wider spectrum of individuals who could potentially fly in low Earth orbit.

Going to the Moon was an extraordinary event in my life. It helped me appreciate this beautiful planet we live on and care about its future. From space I had a rare glimpse of Earth as a small globe in its galactic setting, and I realized that was my *home*. I feel so fortunate I became a space explorer, and I know our future depends on young people who also wish to head out into the unknown and discover new information about our world and universe.

Sometimes when I think back on my life and the many incredible experiences I've had, I feel very happy with what I've accomplished and very appreciative of the people who helped me along the way. It's hard to imagine that a farm boy from a small town in New Mexico could grow up and fly a quarter of a million miles to the Moon and actually get to walk on it. But it really happened.

And what an incredible adventure it was.

Key Life Events

. . . .

1930 Edgar Dean Mitchell is born in Hereford, Texas, on September 17

1934 First ride in an airplane at the age of four aboard a Curtiss JN-4 "Jenny" biplane

1935 Mitchell family moves to New Mexico to farm and raise cattle

1944 Flying lessons at the Artesia, New Mexico, municipal airport and flying solo at 14 in a Piper J-3 Cub prop plane

1946 Earns pilot license at 16

1948 Heads to Carnegie Institute of Technology (Carnegie Mellon) in Pittsburgh, Pennsylvania, to study industrial management

1951   Marries Louise Randall, an art student at Carnegie Tech, on December 21

1952   Graduates from Carnegie Institute of Technology with a bachelor of science degree in industrial management

1952   Enlists in the US Navy

1954   Completes US Navy flight training and is a pilot during the Korean War

1957   After learning about *Sputnik 1*, the world's first satellite launched into space, decides to become a space explorer

1959   Is accepted into the Naval Postgraduate School in Monterey, California, to study aeronautics

1961   Earns a bachelor of science in aeronautics from the US Naval Postgraduate School in Monterey, California

1961   Heads to the Massachusetts Institute of Technology (MIT) in Cambridge, Massachusetts, to study aeronautics and astronautics

1964   Graduates from MIT with a doctor of science in aeronautics and astronautics

1964   Assigned as technical director/navy liaison at the Manned Orbiting Laboratory Program in Los Angeles, California

1965   Trains to become a test pilot at Edwards Air Force Base with legendary pilot Charles Yeager

1966   Selected for NASA Astronaut Corps at the Manned Spacecraft Center in Houston, Texas

1969   Member of the Astronaut Support Crew for Apollo 9

1969   Backup Lunar Module Pilot for Apollo 10

1970   Received the Presidential Medal of Freedom for his help in the rescue of the Apollo 13 crew

1971   Lunar Module Pilot for Apollo 14, which launched January 31

1971   Sixth man to walk on the Moon. Walked on the Moon February 5 and 6, 1971, with Alan Shepard

1971   Received the NASA Distinguished Service Medal for the Apollo 14 mission from President Nixon at a White House ceremony

1971   Received three NASA Group Achievement Awards for exemplary service in the Apollo program

1972   Backup Lunar Module Pilot for Apollo 16

1972   Retired from NASA

1972   Retired from the US Navy as a captain

1973   Founded the Institute of Noetic Sciences

1974   Author of *Psychic Exploration: A Challenge for Science*

1979   Inducted into the Space Hall of Fame

1984   Cofounded the Association of Space Explorers

1996   Author of *The Way of the Explorer: An Apollo Astronaut's Journey Through the Material and Mystical Worlds*

1997   Inducted into the Astronaut Hall of Fame

2005   Nominated for the Nobel Peace Prize

2011   Inducted into the Leonardo da Vinci Society for the Study of Thinking

2012   Author of *The Space Less Traveled: Straight Talk from Apollo 14 Astronaut Edgar Mitchell,* compiled by Carol Mersch

Resources to Explore

. . . .

Websites About Space

Apollo 14 Lunar Surface Journal
www.hq.nasa.gov/alsj/a14/

Discovery News—Space
www.news.discovery.com/space

Edgar Mitchell—Apollo 14
www.edmitchellapollo14.com

Exploring Space—The Quest for Life/PBS
www.pbs.org/exploringspace

Hubblesite—Out of the Ordinary . . . Out of this World
www.hubblesite.org

Kepler—A Search for Habitable Planets
www.kepler.nasa.gov

NASA—Apollo Missions
www.nasa.gov/mission_pages/apollo

NASA—Apollo 14
www.nasa.gov/mission_pages/apollo/missions/apollo14
.html

NASA Kids' Club
www.nasa.gov/audience/forkids/kidsclub/flash/index.html

NASA—Mars Exploration Program
http://mars.jpl.nasa.gov/programmissions

NASA—National Aeronautics and Space Administration
www.nasa.gov

National Geographic—Solar System
http://science.nationalgeographic.com/science/space
/solar-system

Museums and Organizations

Association of Space Explorers
600 Gemini Avenue
Houston, TX 77058
(281) 280-8172
www.space-explorers.org

Astronaut Scholarship Foundation
State Road 405
Kennedy Space Center, FL 32899
(321) 449-4876
www.astronautscholarship.org

Goddard Space Flight Center
8800 Greenbelt Road
Greenbelt, MD 20771
(301) 286-2000
www.nasa.gov/centers/goddard/visitor/home

Infinity Science Center
One Discovery Circle
Stennis Space Center, MS 39529
(228) 533-9025
www.visitinfinity.com

Institute of Noetic Sciences
625 2nd Street, Suite 200
Petaluma, CA 94952-5120
(707) 775-3500
www.noetic.org

International UFO Museum and Research Center
114 North Main Street
Roswell, NM 88203
(800) 822-3545
www.roswellufomuseum.com

Kennedy Space Center
State Road 405
Kennedy Space Center, FL 32899
(866) 737-5235
www.kennedyspacecenter.com

New Mexico Museum of Space History
3198 State Route 2001
Alamogordo, NM 88310
(575) 437-2840
www.nmspacemuseum.org

San Diego Air & Space Museum
2001 Pan American Plaza
San Diego, CA 92101
(619) 234-8291
www.sandiegoairandspace.org

Smithsonian National Air and Space Museum
Independence Avenue at 6th Street, SW
Washington, DC 20560
(202) 633-2214
www.airandspace.si.edu

Space Center Houston
1601 NASA Parkway
Houston, TX 77058
(281) 244-2100
www.spacecenter.org

Space Walk of Fame Museum
4 Main Street
Titusville, FL 32796
(321) 264-0434
www.spacewalkoffame.com

US Space & Rocket Center
One Tranquility Base
Huntsville, AL 35805
(800) 637-7223
www.rocketcenter.com

Walker Aviation Museum
1 Jerry Smith Circle
Roswell, NM 88203
(575) 347-2464
www.wafbmuseum.org

Films and Videos

Apollo 13
This motion picture dramatizes the true story of the 1970 Apollo 13 mission that had a severe spacecraft malfunction. The Apollo crew used their Lunar Module as a lifeboat to safely return to Earth. Release date: 1995

From the Earth to the Moon
Based on author Andrew Chaikin's book, *A Man on the Moon*, this informative 12-part HBO television series highlights the Apollo Moon missions. Release date: 1998

In the Shadow of the Moon
A documentary about the Apollo manned lunar missions in the late 1960s and early 1970s. Apollo astronauts, including Edgar Mitchell, tell their stories in their own words. Release date: 2007

Magnificent Desolation: Walking on the Moon 3D
An IMAX 3D documentary about the 12 men who walked on the Moon. The film title comes from Apollo 11 Astronaut Buzz Aldrin's description of the lunar surface. Release date: 2005

October Sky
The true story of Homer Hickam, a coal miner's son who started to build rockets after he was inspired by the launch of Sputnik 1 in October 1957. Release date: 1999

The Right Stuff
Adapted from author Tom Wolfe's 1979 book, *The Right Stuff*, this film of the same name features the test pilots, such as Edgar Mitchell, who flew high-speed, experimental jets at Edwards Air Force Base in California. Release date: 1983

The Wright Brothers
A feature-length film about Orville and Wilbur Wright, two American brothers/inventors who flew the first "heavier than air" vehicle. Their flight was made at Kitty Hawk, North Carolina, in 1903. Release date: 1997

Wonders of the Solar System
An award-winning television series with five episodes that focus on different aspects of the solar system. The series was produced by the BBC and the Science Channel and hosted by physicist Dr. Brian Cox. Release date: 2010

Wonders of the Universe
A television series with four episodes focusing on different aspects of the universe, produced by the BBC, Discovery Channel, and Science Channel. Also hosted by physicist Dr. Brian Cox. Release date: 2011

Books for Further Reading

Almost Astronauts: 13 Women Who Dared to Dream
By Tanya Lee Stone (Candlewick Press, 2009)
This book tells the story of 13 women in the early years of NASA who were courageous pioneers of the Space Age.

Amelia Lost: The Life and Disappearance of Amelia Earhart
By Candace Fleming (Schwartz & Wade Books, 2011)
This book tells the interesting life story of early aviator Amelia Earhart.

Buck Rogers in the 25th Century:
The Complete Newspaper Dailies: Volume One 1929–1930
The Dille Family Trust (Hermes Press, 2008)
Buck Rogers' fans will find this comprehensive book fascinating and informative.

First Man: The Life of Neil A. Armstrong
By James R. Hansen (Simon & Schuster, 2005)
A book for older readers about Apollo 11 Astronaut Neil Armstrong, who was the first man to walk on the Moon.

Flying to the Moon: An Astronaut's Story
By Michael Collins (Farrar, Straus and Giroux, 1994)
Written by Apollo 11 Astronaut Michael Collins, who was Command Module Pilot and orbited the Moon as Neil Armstrong and Buzz Aldrin walked on the Moon.

Life on Earth and Beyond: An Astrobiologist's Quest
By Pamela S. Turner (Charlesbridge, 2008)
This book looks at the subject of astrobiology, the study of life in the universe.

Look to the Stars
By Buzz Aldrin (Putnam, 2009)
Written for a younger audience, *Look to the Stars* is an informative book written by Buzz Aldrin, the second astronaut to walk on the Moon.

Mission Control, This is Apollo:
The Story of the First Voyages to the Moon
By Andrew Chaikin and Victoria Kohl
(Viking Penguin Group, 2009)
A book about the Moon missions with colorful illustrations and graphics, and dynamic text.

Mission to the Moon
By Alan Dyer (Simon & Schuster
Books for Young People, 2008)
With 200 photos from the NASA archives, this is a visually powerful and informative book about the Moon missions.

My Life as an Astronaut
By Alan Bean (Pocket Books, a division of
Simon & Schuster, 1988)
Apollo 12 Astronaut Alan Bean talks about his life and jour-
ney to the Moon in 1969. Bean, who was the Lunar Module
Pilot for Apollo 12, traveled to the Moon with Commander
Pete Conrad. Bean was the fourth man to walk on the Moon
and is an accomplished artist who has created many paintings
about the Apollo landings.

One Giant Leap: The Story of Neil Armstrong
By Don Brown (Houghton Mifflin, 1998)
A book for young readers about Apollo 11 astronaut Neil Arm-
strong, who was the first man to walk on the Moon.

Rocket Man: The Mercury Adventure of John Glenn
By Rush Ashby (Peachtree Publishers, 2004)
A book about John Glenn, the first American astronaut to
orbit Earth.

Space Rocks: The Story of Planetary Geologist Adriana Ocampo
By Lorraine Jean Hopping (Franklin Watts, 2005)
An interesting look at geologist Adriana Ocampo, who studies
"Moon-like" rocks on Earth to learn more about the universe.

Team Moon: How 400,000 People Landed Apollo 11 on the Moon
By Catherine Thimmesh (Houghton Mifflin, 2006)
Another visually dynamic book about the many people behind
the scenes working on Apollo 11.

The Hubble Space Telescope
By Margaret W. Carruthers (Franklin Watts, 2003)
A comprehensive book about the large Hubble Space
Telescope.

The Man Who Went to the Far Side of the Moon:
The Story of Apollo 11 Astronaut Michael Collins
By Bea Uusma Schyffert (Chronicle Books, 2003)
For younger readers, this colorful book features a scrapbook style with illustrations, photographs, and text. It highlights the story of Apollo 11 Astronaut Michael Collins, who flew the Columbia Command Module above the lunar surface, as well as Neil Armstrong and Buzz Aldrin, who took the very first steps on the Moon in 1969.

To Space and Back
By Sally Ride with Susan Okie
(Lothrop, Lee & Shepard Books, 1986)
Astronaut Sally Ride, an American physicist, was the first American woman to enter space. In this book Sally Ride describes living and working in the space shuttle while orbiting Earth.

Wonders of the Universe
By Dr. Brian Cox and Andrew Cohen
(HarperCollins Publishers, 2011)
A highly fascinating, visual, and informative look at the mysteries of the universe.

Index

····················